Routledge Revivals

The European Community in the World

First published in 1973 *The European Community in the World* shows what 'outward looking' can mean in terms of British participation in the Community and of the Community's policies and actions as a world power. Richard Bailey says that the time for argument for or against British membership of the Common market has gone. The enlargement of the Community is a fact: how, then, can Britain best adjust to the new situation? The extension of the European Community is significant for all the world and will increase its power among the institutions that govern the world, affecting the politics of many countries from Sweden to Swaziland.

In post Brexit world, this book is a must read for students and scholars of European politics, European history, British history, and British politics.

The European Community in
the World

Richard Bailey

Routledge
Taylor & Francis Group

First published in 1973
by Hutchinson & Co

This edition first published in 2023 by Routledge
4 Park Square, Milton Park, Abingdon, Oxon, OX14 4RN

and by Routledge
605 Third Avenue, New York, NY 10017

Routledge is an imprint of the Taylor & Francis Group, an informa business

© Richard Bailey 1973

Publisher's Note
The publisher has gone to great lengths to ensure the quality of this reprint but points out that some imperfections in the original copies may be apparent.

Disclaimer
The publisher has made every effort to trace copyright holders and welcomes correspondence from those they have been unable to contact.

A Library of Congress record exists under ISBN: 0091187214

ISBN: 978-1-032-50940-2 (hbk)
ISBN: 978-1-003-40036-3 (ebk)
ISBN: 978-1-032-50943-3 (pbk)

Book DOI 10.4324/9781003400363

The European Community in the World

RICHARD BAILEY

HUTCHINSON OF LONDON

Hutchinson & Co (Publishers) Ltd
3 Fitzroy Square, London W 1

London Melbourne Sydney Auckland
Wellington Johannesburg Cape Town
and agencies throughout the world

First published 1973
© Richard Bailey 1973

Set in 'Monotype' Times

Printed in Great Britain by
W & J Mackay Limited, Chatham
and bound by B. F. Hardwick Ltd,
Shipley, Yorkshire

ISBN 0 09 118720 6 (cased)

ISBN 0 09 118721 4 (paperback)

Contents

Contents

Preface

This book has been written in the belief that the time for expressing views for or against British membership of the Common Market has now gone by. The enlargement of the Community is a fact of UK political and economic life and we should be turning our attention to ways and means of adjusting to the new situation. In no field is this more important than in external relationships. From its base in Europe the Community has extended its influence geographically and politically through its economic policies, especially CAP, and by the negotiation of trading arrangements with a host of associates which now include many Commonwealth countries. The present and future impact of this extended Community is the theme of this book.

I should like to thank the various individuals who have helped me to collect and sift the material presented here, while holding them in no way responsible for the use I have made of it.

Westminster   Richard Bailey

List of Abbreviations

AASM   Association of African States and Malagasy
(the eighteen Yaounde Convention signatories)

Benelux Belgium, Netherlands, Luxembourg Customs Union
BTN   Brussels Tariff Nomenclature

CAP   Common Agricultural Policy
CET   Common External Tariff (of EC)
CFA   Communauté Française Africaine

DAC   Development Assistance Committee (OECD)

EC   European Community
ECSC   European Coal and Steel Community (part of
European Community)
EDF   European Development Fund (of EC)
EEC   European Economic Community (part of European
Community)
EFTA   European Free Trade Association
Euratom European Atomic Energy Authority
(part of European Community)

FEOGA   Agricultural Guarantee and Guidance Fund (of EC)

GATT   General Agreement on Tariffs and Trade
GDR   German Democratic Republic (East Germany)
GSP   Generalized System of Preferences

IBRD   International Bank for Reconstruction and

	Development (the World Bank)
IMF	International Monetary Fund
NATO	North Atlantic Treaty Organization
OECD	Organization for Economic Cooperation and Development (Paris)
OPEC	Organization of Petroleum Exporting Countries
UNCTAD	United Nations Conference on Trade and Development

Introduction: The Extended Community

British membership of the Common Market has tended to be discussed in terms of its impact on the cost of living, employment, the social services, education and other aspects of our internal situation, enlivened on the political front by laments at the diminished importance of the British Parliament. At workaday level the discussion has come down to the price of food, especially butter, the size of their juggernauts compared with ours, wage-rates here and on the Continent, and the complexities of VAT. Very little has been heard of the opposite question of how the addition of Britain, Ireland and Denmark has affected the Community. How far in fact is enlargement a process of the Six absorbing the new members and fitting them into an established system, and how far one of creating a new Community in order to take them on board? Clearly both processes are involved. The negotiations provided for the new members to adopt the rules, procedures and common policies of the Six by the end of an agreed transition period. This process has not only affected the domestic policies of the new entrants but also produced an enlarged Community which is different in a number of ways from the old six-member model.

The most significant difference between the nine-member Community and its predecessor is in external relations. The enlargement of the European Community is not simply a matter of adding three new members and remembering to talk about the Nine instead of the Six. By the middle of 1977, Britain will be part of an extended Community which will include the EFTA non-joiners, the Mediterranean countries, the French-speaking African states, and a host of Commonwealth countries which take up the option of associate membership. Put together in a coherent relationship this miscellany of associates adds a new dimension to the European

Community.

But in fact the value of British membership cannot be judged on the experience of one or even nine nations. The logic of joining the EC rests not on Continental economics but on the fact that the Six were in process of re-organizing Europe and deciding its place within the world economy. If Britain's international importance now rests on her experience and skill in world trade and in the continuance of the Commonwealth connection, then clearly it is important that she should be involved in this process. What has not been generally realized is that the emergence of an enlarged Community has passed beyond the stage of being a European activity. The Six had already formed special relationships with African and Mediterranean countries and with various non-member states in Europe, so that even before the accession of Britain an extended Community was in process of being formed. The United States administration has pointed out at intervals that the Six were setting up an area of trade discrimination in conflict with GATT rules. The European Common Market of six nations was created as a permitted exception to the GATT non-discrimination rule, as was the EFTA. The host of special arrangements that have been added on to what was itself an exception to the rules has contributed to the problems of the GATT and the IMF. The result is that the Bretton Woods institutions now have to be overhauled, not because three new members have joined the Community, but because an extended Community of over fifty members is in process of formation.

The extended Community, like the extended family of the sociologists, has the effect of widening the influence of the core group, in this case the Nine. The cousins, aunts, uncles, in-laws and so on of the extended family are paralleled by the associates and dependencies of the Community. They have in common a connection with the Community which distinguishes them from non-members. This connection may be only one aspect of their external relations but it is nevertheless distinctive and therefore significant.

THE FACTS OF MEMBERSHIP

How does the formation of the extended Community affect Britain's position? As a member of the European Community, Britain's overseas relationships have to be carried out within a framework laid down in the Treaty of Accession derived mainly from previous Community policies, with certain concessions to British commitments. The fact of membership has to be accepted and it serves no useful purpose to look at problems of Community relationships in terms of the 1950s and 1960s. The 'great' debate over joining or staying out trotted out the old arguments used in 1963, combining updated figures and outdated attitudes. In effect Britain had a straight choice of joining and adjusting to a Europe dominated by the Community on the inside, or staying out and trying to establish a viable position on the perimeter.

This choice was set out in the 1971 White Paper* in the following way:

> The strength and prosperity of the United Kingdom depend partly on the efforts of its peoples, and partly on the economic conditions prevailing in the world outside. We live, and have for long lived, by manufacturing for and trading with that world. The conditions under which we manufacture and trade are all of vital national interest to us. We have to consider whether these conditions will be more favourable to us if we join the European Communities than if we do not. (Part One paragraph 3.)

The possibility of making such a choice created the prospect of a fresh start. The ineffectiveness of British economic policy throughout the 1960s had brought a growing awareness that in an era of change we were in danger of becoming one of the world's museum pieces. The Commonwealth, although, as will be argued later, an important force in focusing the great issues of race relations and the economic development of the Third World, has moved into a new phase where Britain, as one of its thirty-two full members, is as likely, or unlikely, to be expelled as any of the others. It can be argued therefore that if Britain needs the Community the Community also needs Britain. In the words of the 1971 White Paper, 'it is for question whether the Communities without the United Kingdom can be as secure and prosperous as they need to be in the modern world. The entry of the United Kingdom into the European Communities is therefore an issue of historic importance, not only for us, but for Europe, and for the world.' (Part One para. 5.)†

* *The United Kingdom and the European Communities,* Cmnd. 4715.
† The White Paper refers to the three Communities making up the European

The negotiations for joining the European Community consisted of three main parts. The first covered the acceptance of the political and economic provisions of the Rome Treaty, together with the various related measures agreed since the EEC came into being on 1 January 1958, which are covered by Secondary Legislation. Second it involved accepting and taking part in agreements made by the EEC with third countries including the AASM (Association of African States and Malagasy – the eighteen Francophone states). Thirdly the Treaty contained provisions for special arrangements with the Commonwealth countries, and with the EFTA non-applicants. The object of the negotiations was to bring in the three new members with the minimum of alteration to the Rome Treaty and with special arrangements, e.g. for agriculture, confined to a

Diagram 1. Tariffs at the Starting Point

Average Tariff Rates After Kennedy Round Reductions		Percentage Reduction in Kennedy Round	
Manufactured and Semi-manufactured Products (Weighted by OECD Trade)		Total trade	Total mfg.
United States	Average Rate 8.3%	32	38
European Community	Average Rate 8.4%	32	36
United Kingdom	Average Rate 10.2%	35	38
Japan	Average Rate 10.9%	25	40
Canada	Average Rate Estimated between 10% and 12%		

Community – the EEC, European Coal and Steel Community and Euratom, all of which are covered by the Treaty of Accession.

transitional period. In other words the Community was enlarged on the basis of the existing Treaties and their political objectives. Any changes in accepted procedures and policies which come later will be the result of agreement between the Nine. The Community can make proposals for association or trading arrangements which the countries concerned can accept or reject.

The picture of the Six (or Nine) concentrating on internal European problems to the exclusion of their wider interests outside is not a true image of Community life. Certainly the 'inward-looking' aspects of the Common Agricultural Policy (CAP) use up a lot of time and resources, but CAP cannot be considered only in European terms but in its relations to GATT, international commodity agreements and world trade in agricultural products. The same is true of different applications of industrial and commercial policy.

The extension of the Community to include a selection of Commonwealth countries, while excluding others, is significant on a global rather than a European plane. It creates difficulties for the international institutions dealing with trade, aid and monetary arrangements. It interposes a new organizational layer between the IMF, World Bank and GATT and the national governments. It introduces the further division among the developing countries, already categorized as French- or English-speaking, of 'associables' or 'non-associables'. The effect of the Treaty is to create a Community Africa and a non-associable India and Latin America. Whether this is a better arrangement than one in which no developing countries have special associations with a particular group of developed countries is impossible to say. It is however part of a situation which has been brought about by the enlargement of the Community. In international terms, the Community has extended its influence into the province of the global institutions and affected the external relations of a wide array of countries ranging from Sweden to Swaziland. Within Europe Britain, with shades of her world power past about her, is the odd one out among Community members. In considering the role and importance of the Community in the world and the effect of its extension beyond Europe, Britain may be well placed to initiate and guide future development. But it is British membership that has in fact precipitated changes in the operation of the global institutions which were

14

perhaps already overdue, but which would certainly not otherwise have come so quickly. The Brussels negotiations of 1971–2 must be seen as the prelude to a series of adjustments in political and commercial relationships between the nations of the world, developed and developing alike.

ADJUSTMENTS ALL ROUND

As a result of membership of the European Community, Britain is in a situation in which her external relationships all require modification. In Europe, joining the Community involves leaving EFTA and taking up a new position of association with Greece and Turkey. In the Commonwealth, the independent members have been divided into associables with options for getting into the Community act, non-associables which are excluded from it, and countries for which special transitional arrangements have been made. In relation to the United States, Britain's position is clearer in that the old 'special' relationship is over and we are now part of a joint Community position. From regarding the Community as an essential component of the world monetary and trading arrangements, the Americans have come round to the view that they have been left to carry the economic burdens while the Six worked away at integration. They are inclined to blame the breakdown of the Bretton Woods system on the European Community and insist that it must share responsibility for putting something else in its place. Britain, at last free of the responsibilities of operating a reserve currency and preoccupied with domestic economic problems, has tended to float independently both in a currency and a European policy sense.

The enlargement of the Community has therefore come at a time when a new approach to world economic arrangements has become necessary. How far this situation is the result of the action or inaction of the Six, or of the difficulties due to trying to accommodate Britain and the Commonwealth in a preferential trading system, is a matter for discussion. What is clear is that a new approach to world monetary and trading arrangements has now to be made as a matter of urgency.

The other aspect of Britain's external relations which has changed is the position of the Commonwealth. Of the thirty-two

independent members, twenty have the option of a form of asso-
ciate membership. With Malta and Cyprus already associates and
Britain a full member, this means that only nine independent
Commonwealth countries are outside the extended Community.
They include the three developed countries Australia, Canada and
New Zealand, as well as India, Malaysia, Sri Lanka and Singapore.
This raises several important questions. How will this division
affect relationships within the Commonwealth? What will be the
impact on Britain's relationship with developing countries gener-
ally? How will the associables relate to the Community? Will
Britain's preoccupation with Community-oriented arrangements
mean a loosening of ties with countries outside this charmed
circle?

WHERE NEXT?

At the Summit meeting in the Hague at the end of 1969, the Six
agreed to open membership negotiations with Britain and the other
candidates and at the same time to press forward with measures to
'complete, deepen and enlarge the Community'. As a result the
three new members have been admitted but the search for a Community rationale continues. There is a famous cartoon by Max
Beerbohm which shows Tennyson reading his poems to Queen
Victoria, who is inquiring, 'But what were they going to do with
the Holy Grail when they'd found it, Mr Tennyson?' This is
exactly the position as the Nine line up to build an enlarged Community in Western Europe's rich and affluent land. In the 1970s the
call to unite Europe is no longer so potent as it was in the days
when the Monnet idea was hailed as a brilliant response to the
need for new policies for a jaded continent. Now the enlarged
Community is a fact, it exists with its refurbished but not reformed institutions ready to help solve the problems of the decade.
What will now count is the extent to which by solving national
problems, such as how to combat regional unemployment, it will
enable governments to combine their efforts at Community level
to attack the problems of the developing countries, replace the
Bretton Woods system, and so on. Some national problems may
in future be passed upwards for solution at Community level,
others will be decentralized with the hope that, in a wider context,

16

it will be possible to engage the individual once more in the process of government. But these preoccupations must not divert attention from the basic fact that the role of the Community as a world power remains to be worked out. Is it to take its place as one of the world's five major powers alongside the United States, the USSR, China and Japan? Or is it to be the channel for organizing the West European Region within the framework of re-organized global institutions? What happens to the Commonwealth with some of its members associated with the Community and some, including India, outside it? Can a group of nations as wide-ranging as the extended Community be regarded as being in any true sense regional? Or does it by its size and geographical spread constitute a rival to the institutions of the Bretton Woods system?

These are the sort of questions that have been lurking on the edge of Common Market discussions. The decision to hold the GATT negotiations in the autumn of 1973 had the effect of bringing them into the open. During the long waiting period before Britain eventually managed to become a member, the concept of the 'outward-looking' Community was often spoken of, but never defined or developed. This book attempts to show what 'outward-looking' means in terms of British participation in the Community, and of the Community's policies and actions on the world stage.

1. The Community in Europe

If the enlarged Community is to make sense in a European context it must be seen in relation to the objectives of the 1970s. The 1960s in spite of the internal conflict between French and Community interests, saw the realization of the basic objectives of the Rome Treaty, with the creation of the Customs Union and the implementation of the Common Agricultural Policy. At that time the Six were working to a blueprint which set out clearly what they had to do. Now this part of the operation is finished, and there is no comparable guidance for action in the decade ahead. Britain and the other new entrants have arrived on the scene at a time when discussions of principles and new policy formation will be high on the agenda. These discussions will determine policies for a Community which is based in Europe but international in influence and character.

Within Europe the enlargement of the Community marks the end of the debate on unification which went on in the late 1950s and 1960s. With the United Kingdom as a member, and EFTA in its old form wound up, the Community is now the unique focus of political and economic power in Western Europe. The growing interdependence of the economies of the industrial states means that many problems previously dealt with by national governments now have to be considered in a wider context. In so far as a European approach to international trading and monetary problems is required, there will increasingly be a Community line with which the non-member states of Western Europe will go along. For this reason the key requirement now is not to 'unite' Europe but to establish working relationships of various kinds that enable members of the Community to act together as a European power,

18

and associate non-members with this task in a role appropriate to their situation and requirements.

FITTING IN EFTA

Of the adjustments that had to be made, the most important concerned the 'non-joiners' among the former European Free Trade Association countries. EFTA was formed by seven states which for one reason or another had come to the conclusion that they could not join the European Economic Community. Its role of alternative group ended when Britain, Denmark and Norway (later to fall by the wayside) decided that they could join the Community and negotiated terms accordingly. The nature of these two sets of decisions, the first taken in May 1960, the second implemented on 1 January 1973, emphasizes the second-best, provisional character of EFTA. The establishment of EEC in 1958 made it inevitable that the non-members would need some kind of organization for joint action. If the 1971–2 negotiations had failed, as did those of 1963 and 1967, it is probable that EFTA would have continued on its useful but unglamorous way for a further period.

However, it would be wrong to assume that EFTA was no more than a political *poste restante*, a convenience for those of its members who expected one day to be changing their address from Geneva to Brussels. At the beginning it was an association of countries that were not ready to join a fully-fledged economic union but preferred cooperation and free trade on a flexible basis, without rules, and with no common policies or elaborate central institutions. In 1960 the seven, Austria, Switzerland, Denmark, Norway, Sweden, Portugal and Britain, were demonstrating that free trade could be made to work, but no one would pretend that EFTA would have appeared on the European scene if the EEC had not arrived first. Its members had all taken part in the abortive negotiations for a European Free Trade Area in 1958–9, and having been rejected by the Six decided that they needed an organization to give each other support during the period of waiting before Western Europe was eventually united. Of the varied assortment of international bodies operating in Europe in the 1960s, few can have given better service to their members than EFTA.

HOW EFTA WORKED

The Stockholm Convention of 4 January 1960* set out precise provisions for the removal of tariffs and quotas on industrial goods, and defined specific rules of origin. The practical objective was to establish an organization with a minimum of rules and regulations, capable of operation by a small secretariat. The removal of tariffs on trade in industrial goods between members was originally due for completion in 1970, but the deadline was moved forward so that the process was complete at the end of 1966. The EFTA Agreement covered manufactured goods and excluded agriculture. Exceptions to the general elimination of industrial tariffs were introduced for 'sensitive' industries in some countries, and to help Portugal, the most backward of the member states, to adapt its economy to free trade. The major problem was to institute a workable system to deal with deflection of trade in the absence of a common external tariff. Without some appropriate mechanism it would have been possible, for example, for American cars imported into Denmark over a twelve per cent tariff to be re-exported to Britain, so escaping a large part of the twenty-five per cent tariff there. The answer to this problem was found in the rules of origin, which provided the basis on which goods qualified for EFTA tariff treatment. To be considered as made in EFTA, goods had to contain less than fifty per cent in value of non-EFTA, that is imported, materials, or else have undergone certain manufacturing processes in an EFTA country. These alternatives were known as the 'value' and 'process' criteria. It was open to manufacturers to choose whichever criterion was appropriate as the grounds for claiming tariff exemption.

The governing body of EFTA, the Council, consisted of representatives of the governments of the seven member countries. Relations with Finland, an associate member, were dealt with by the joint council of EFTA and Finland. Iceland only became a member of EFTA in 1970. The Council met two or three times a year, but meetings of heads of permanent delegations were held in Geneva every week. Various standing committees dealt with customs, technical problems connected with EFTA trade, financial

* *Convention Establishing the European Free Trade Association*, HMSO Cmnd. 1026.

20

problems, and trade in agricultural products. In addition the Economic Development Committee, Consultative Committee and Economic Committee kept problems of economic integration under review.

EFTA TRADE

The abolition of tariffs creates new conditions and new opportunities. In particular in a free trade area it gives rise to two effects known as 'trade creation' and 'trade diversion'. The former effect is defined as that part of new trade which replaces actual or potential home production. This is regarded as a benefit because it involves the substitution of low-cost imports from within the area for high-cost domestic products. It is both an import benefit for the importing country and an export benefit for the country producing the substituted goods. The second effect, 'trade diversion', comes about when members of a free trade area change some of their sources of supply, buying from inside the group rather than from former outside suppliers. The development of EFTA trade has been analysed in two major studies. The first was published by the EFTA council in January 1969, under the title 'The Effects of EFTA on the Economies of Member States'. It showed that by 1965, the year by which EFTA had completed about three quarters of the tariff abolition process, trade creation had brought more gains in trade to EFTA countries than they had lost through trade diversion. The second study, published in June 1972 under the title 'The Trade Effects of EFTA and EEC', examined the effects of the creation of EFTA and the EEC on the economies of the members of both groups.

It has often been argued that splitting Europe into two groups had harmful effects on the economies of their members which have outweighed the benefits gained. The EFTA study showed that all the member countries gained more in exports from participation in either EFTA or EEC than they lost from discrimination against their trade by the other group. In general, more EEC exports were diverted from the EFTA market than the reverse, but the EEC had a greater impact on intra-EEC exports. In both groups the gain in trade between members outweighed losses in exports to the other group, so that there was a net rise in total exports. Even for the

21

United Kingdom the loss in exports to the Six, due to the creation of the EEC, was small compared with the gains registered in British exports to other EFTA countries. While both EFTA and the EEC were successful in creating new trade, it does not follow that the division of Europe into two blocs was beneficial. In both cases there was a relatively high cost in trade diversion between groups which would not have occurred in a single large market.

JOINING THE COMMUNITY

The decision of Britain, Norway and Denmark to join the European Community meant that the 'non-joiners', Austria, Switzerland, Portugal, Sweden, Finland, Iceland and, as events turned out, Norway, were also forced to consider their future relationship with the EEC. Although not seeking membership, all of them hoped to establish clear economic and trading relations with the Community. Negotiations on the basis of a mandate approved by the Council of Ministers opened in November 1971 and separate talks with the individual governments were held later. The object of the negotiations was stated to be to resolve problems facing the six non-joiners arising from the enlargement of the Community, and to secure the growth of their trade and establish economic relations with it.

The varying levels of development of the countries involved inevitably created problems. Portugal with its large farming population and lower level of industrialization required an extended programme for tariff reductions. For Finland the problem was to maintain a competitive trading position without prejudicing its neutrality by any political involvement in the development of the institutions of the Community. Austria and Switzerland were prepared to enter into a wide-ranging economic relationship with the Community and the former agreed to include trade in agricultural produce in the negotiations. Sweden favoured a customs union between itself and the Community, along with a common agricultural policy, and was prepared to put its relations with the Community on an institutional basis and take part in its decision-making process, cooperate in monetary and industrial policies and economic planning, and accept Community rules for price competition and state aids for industry. Iceland, the smallest and

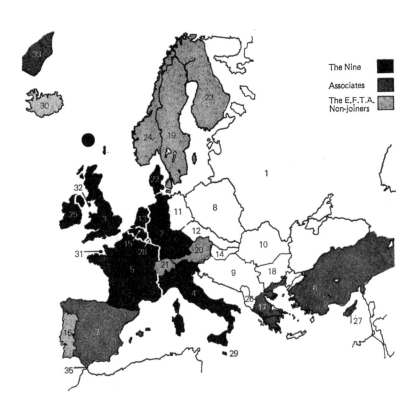

The Nine			■
Associates			■
The E.F.T.A. Non-joiners			░

1 USSR	10 Romania	19 Sweden	28 Luxembourg
2 Germany, Fed. Rep. of	11 Germany (Eastern)	20 Austria	29 Malta
3 United Kingdom	12 Czechoslovakia	21 Switzerland	30 Iceland
4 Italy	13 Netherlands	22 Denmark	31 Channel Islands
5 France	14 Hungary	23 Finland	32 Isle of Man
6 Turkey	15 Belgium	24 Norway	33 Greenland
7 Spain	16 Portugal	25 Ireland	34 Faeroe Islands
8 Poland	17 Greece	26 Albania	35 Gibraltar
9 Yugoslavia	18 Bulgaria	27 Cyprus	

The Community in Europe

Diagram 2. GNP at the starting point

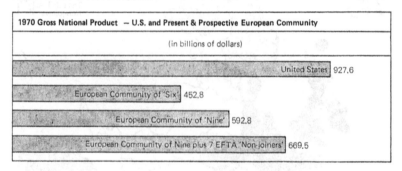

1970 Gross National Product — U.S. and Present & Prospective European Community

(in billions of dollars)

United States 927.6

European Community of 'Six' 452.8

European Community of 'Nine' 592.8

European Community of Nine plus 7 EFTA 'Non-joiners' 669.5

newest EFTA member, was anxious to continue selling its fish in the enlarged Community, an aim which has not been helped by the decision to extend its fishing limits to fifty miles.

THE FIVE AGREEMENTS

On 22 July 1972 the five EFTA non-joiners – Austria, Iceland, Portugal, Sweden and Switzerland – signed free trade agreements with the European Communities. Although negotiated bilaterally on the basis of the different national priorities indicated above, the agreements shared many articles in common. Finland, an associate of EFTA, negotiated a similar agreement which was ratified some time later.

The agreements between the enlarged Community and the EFTA non-joiners came into force on 1 January 1973, with the exception of Norway, which had fallen out of step with the negotiations as a result of the 'No' voted in November 1972 in the national referendum on Community membership. The countries affected had a number of objectives in common but it was not possible to fit all of these into a single act as in the case of the Treaty of Accession. In effect therefore a separate treaty was negotiated with each country, taking account of its special circumstances. While the six treaties had many similarities, and all agreed on certain matters, no two were identical.

Each of the agreements had thirteen articles and three protocols, but the wording of these varied and in some cases additional paragraphs were inserted. The three protocols included in all agreements dealt with: (1) sensitive products; (2) processed foodstuffs; (3) rules of origin. In addition all the agreements contained a protocol on Ireland, and four of them included additional protocols on other matters. Finland as a former associate negotiated a separate agreement in a different form which was signed too late for it to become effective on 1 January 1973 at the same time as the others.*

SIX PLUS SEVEN

The most important achievement of the agreements was the preservation of the free trade arrangements existing between the eight original EFTA members and their associate Finland. This meant that British and Danish membership of the Community did not involve them in raising tariff barriers against a group of countries with which they enjoyed free trade. Going on from this, the non-joiners agreed to extend this area of free trade to cover the majority of industrial products traded between the original EFTA countries, the original Six and Ireland. This extension will take place in five stages with tariff reductions of twenty per cent on 1 April yearly from 1973 to 1976, and on 1 July 1977. A slower timetable will apply to sensitive products set out in the protocols to the Agreements and including paper, man-made fibres, special steels, aluminium (unwrought) and various non-ferrous metals (tung-

* Those wishing to check on the details of the agreements should consult EFTA Bulletin Number 8, vol. XIII, November 1972, which sets out the agreement with Switzerland as the master agreement and indicates the differences from this of the other four agreements.

sten, molybdenum, etc.). Portugal has its own list of sensitive products, including cork, and cotton and jute textiles. The existing EFTA rules of origin continued in force until April 1973, after which new rules based on existing Community association and preferential agreements came into operation.

Agricultural products, excluded from the original EFTA agreement, were in the end taken out of the agreements, although the Commission had attempted to secure agricultural concessions from some ex-EFTA countries. The agreements do not provide for any harmonization of policies on Rome Treaty lines. Certain specific practices are however forbidden, where trade under the treaties is adversely affected. These include agreements between firms that distort competition, the abuse of a dominant position, and state aids favouring certain undertakings or the production of particular categories of goods. These echoes of Articles 85 and 86 of the Rome Treaty are accompanied by other measures which reinforce the policy obligations of the agreements. Amongst these are escape and safeguard clauses to cover balance of payments difficulties, dumping, and sectoral and regional problems. There are also safeguard clauses which can be invoked where tariff anomalies get in the way of the free movement of goods. In most cases where escape or safeguard clauses apply the principle of prior consultation between the parties concerned must be followed.

The trading arrangements of the ex-EFTA countries, Austria, Switzerland, Portugal, Sweden, Iceland and Finland, which have not joined the EEC are now in a period of transition. They have free trade with each other in manufactured goods and also, with the United Kingdom and Denmark. All of them are now in process of dismantling tariffs on industrial products traded with the EEC, and will have achieved free trade in this sector by 1 July 1977. The Norwegian government, having failed in its attempt to join the EEC, negotiated an agreement on similar lines to those of the other non-joiners, which came into effect on 14 May 1973. The two countries which depend most heavily on non-industrial products, Portugal and Iceland, have made special provisions, the former for wines, tomato puree and canned foods, and the latter for fish and fish products. Sweden, Switzerland and Austria have agreed to special treatment for imports of wines, fruit, vegetables and flowers from the Community. All the non-joiners except Finland have agreed to an 'evolutionary' clause which enables them to propose the extension of the arrangements made in their agreements to other spheres, subject to the agreement of the Community.

RULES OF ORIGIN

One change of major importance from the procedures of the original EFTA is the introduction of a new system of rules of origin. This is the system already in use by the Community in preferential agreements, so that the ex-EFTA countries are being brought into line, not made a special case of. As the agreements do not provide for a customs union, or contain any general obligation to harmonize legislation, arrangements to ensure the harmonious working of free trade have to be introduced. All industrial goods moving between the sixteen nations covered by the agreements, that is the nine Community members and Austria, Sweden, Switzerland, Portugal, Iceland, Finland and Norway, will have to be covered by a certificate of origin issued by the customs office concerned. The basic rule is that a product originates in a country if it is wholly manufactured there, or if it undergoes processing which changes its tariff position. This means in effect that it moves from a tariff position in which it is treated as a raw material or a semi-processed material to one in which it is treated as a manufactured article. In some cases processing will not all take place within one country. The rule then is that to qualify for a certificate of origin a certain percentage of its value must have been added in the country applying for exemption from duty. The difference from the former EFTA rules of origin is that a distinction is made between Community members and the non-joiners on the question of processing in more than one country. Where raw materials start in one country and undergo processing in two or three others, the increase in value is cumulative. The value added to products by processing in a number of non-joiner countries – for example Swedish timber imported by an Austrian manufacturer – can not be added together to determine origin. Such a calculation is allowed, however, for processing by the nine Community countries. The proportion of value added by processing must not include more than an agreed proportion of third country goods. Examples are fifteen per cent for parts and spares for motor cars, ten per cent for most textiles and chemicals, and three per cent for transistors. These rules or origin will be the same for the enlarged Community and the non-joiner EFTA countries, and will also apply to trade between the non-joiners. In conception and execution they are likely to prove tougher than the old EFTA regulations. However by the time the main programme of tariff cuts is completed in 1977, and Portugal and Iceland have worked out their longer timetable extending to 1 January 1980, there will be an industrial free trade zone of some 300 million people. This is not quite the same thing as the Maudling Committee was trying to set up in 1957, but it is a tremendous advance on anything that has existed in Western Europe before. Nor is this the end of the matter, as the Community has already extended its influence by agreements with other West European nations.

The agreements with the former EFTA countries bring to an end the division of Europe into the Six and the Seven. The evolutionary nature of the agreements allows for changes as the Community develops. This is important because looking ahead no one can say how a nine-member Community will differ from the six-member módel. A number of problems will have to work themselves out during the transitional period. Operating through the old institutional arrangements the EFTA Council will continue to meet during the transitional period, so that Britain and Denmark will remain in close touch with the non-joiners and their problems while adjusting to the rigours of Brussels. After that the six non-joiners may go on working together with a slimmed-down secretariat or they may move into some closer relationship with the European Community. The significant fact about the new situation is that it takes account of the hard practical facts of living alongside the Community. The agreements on paper imports by Britain from Austria, Finland and Sweden, the special consideration for Iceland fish and Portuguese farm products, are all subject to review in 1975. This sort of arrangement may be unglamorous, but getting down to tomato puree and cod roes has been shown to have done more towards uniting Europe than rhetoric and good intentions. One final point which emphasizes the difficulties of integration, the working language of the EFTA non-joiners is English, which is not the native tongue of any of them.

THE REST OF WESTERN EUROPE

The various agreements made with other West European countries had been of relatively minor importance up to the enlargement of the Community on 1 January 1973. None of the countries concerned – Greece, Turkey and Spain – would have been able to take on the responsibilities of full membership of the EEC and face the industrial competition from the Six. All three countries have relatively backward economies with a high proportion of the population engaged in agriculture. None of them was considered for EFTA membership back in 1960. The agreement with Greece dating back to 1961 was suspended in 1967 when the regime of the colonels was established. Since then the agreement has been concerned only with minor trade concessions. Some of the Six, especially the Benelux countries, have always opposed forming an association with Spain on political grounds. Both of these countries, and Turkey, are likely to be involved in the wider agreement in process of being formed with the Mediterranean countries. The association agreements between them and the Six, all of which have to be renegotiated to fit the enlarged Community, are summarized briefly here.

Greece. Negotiations for association between Greece and the Six were initiated on 25 July 1959 and concluded two years later. The agreement, negotiated under Article 238 of the Rome Treaty, provided for the association of Greece with the Six on the basis of a customs union, with the prospect of full membership when her economy was sufficiently developed to assume the same commercial obligations as the Six. The agreement provided for the removal of Greek tariffs on imports from the Community over a period of twelve years, and twenty-two years for industrial goods which represented about one third of Greek imports. Loans from the European Investment Bank (125m. dollars from 1962–7) were promised to help develop the Greek economy. The harmonization of Greek agriculture with that of the Community was agreed, giving the main farm products – tobacco, raisins, olives, fruit and vegetables – equal treatment with those of the Six. Quotas were fixed for Greek wines based on the existing level of exports. The main developments up to 1967 while the Association Agreement

29

was operative were the first tariff reductions on both sides and the granting of more favourable treatment for Greek raisins and tobacco.

Turkey. Turkey became associated with the EEC in a customs union, with provision for eventual full membership, in an agreement which came into force on 1 December 1964. The agreement envisaged three stages of development. The first was the preparatory period of five years during which Turkey was granted tariff quotas in the EEC for tobacco, dried grapes, dried figs and hazel nuts. These four items together accounted for thirty-seven per cent of Turkey's exports. At the same time loans of 175m. dollars from the European Investment Bank for capital projects were granted under a Finance Protocol. In the Second or Transitional Stage, agreed in July 1970 but not ratified and operative until 1 January 1973, plans were made for establishing a customs union with the EEC over a period of twelve years, to cover all trade, with a special system for agriculture to be introduced to fit in with the requirements of the Common Agricultural Policy. When this was completed a third or definitive stage would be inaugurated which would see the achievement of a full customs union, after which Turkey would be eligible to apply for full membership of the Community. An Association Council of members of governments of EEC countries and Turkey, plus some Commission members, supervises the arrangements.

Spain. In the case of Spain the Six showed themselves at first reluctant to open negotiations, and it was not until April 1967 that a start was made in discussing a possible agreement. A two-stage agreement was envisaged, the first to last for six years with a second stage of indeterminate length. The Spanish government sought association partly as an indication that the regime had a degree of acceptance. On the economic front there was anxiety to reduce dependence on tourism and remittances from Spaniards working in other parts of Europe, notably the Federal Republic, and to build up a sound industrial base. The Community eventually signed an agreement with Spain in 1970. This was a six-year preferential trade agreement on the lines that had been discussed at intervals since negotiations had begun in 1967. In accordance with the GATT rules, the agreement contained provision for the formation of a customs union after a reasonable interval. The Community agreed to lower its industrial tariffs by sixty per cent by the beginning of 1977, and a possible further ten per cent after that. A forty per cent tariff-cut on citrus fruit was introduced and provision made for cuts on duties on tomatoes and olive oil. Spain agreed to increase its import quotas on goods from the Community by thirteen per cent a year, with an increase of at least seven per cent on all products. Tariff reductions by Spain of from twenty-five to sixty per cent on three lists of industrial products were also agreed. An 'additional protocol' to adapt the EEC agreement with Spain to the enlarged Community was signed on 29 January 1973. The United Kingdom, Denmark and Ireland will not alter their commercial provisions with Spain until the beginning of 1974 at the earliest. This protocol is a legal device to cover the period until a new agreement might be negotiated. The enlargement of the Community and the special arrangements with the EFTA non-joiners have tended to worsen the position of Spain in Community trade.

The position of the three special cases – Greece, Turkey and Spain – will be discussed further in relation to the Community's Mediterranean policy.

2. The Community Spreads Southwards

The idea that the European Community is in any real sense 'European' begins to appear less credible when its present and future relationships outside the continent of Europe are examined. A sixteen-nation free trade area, nine of whose members form a Common Market, would appear to be logical in a context defined by history and geography rather than economics. When first the Six and then the Nine look outwards from Western Europe and form associations with a miscellany of countries at various stages of development, including some of the poorest in the world, a number of questions arise. First there is the basis of selection. The extension of the former colonial connections of France, Belgium and Holland to developing countries in Africa, the Caribbean and elsewhere was not regarded with favour by those developing countries left out of the arrangement. Does the inclusion of a number of Commonwealth countries, but the exclusion of the greater part of Commonwealth population, make the process of association respectable?

When the Treaty of Accession was negotiated it was established that some twenty Commonwealth countries could be associated with the enlarged Community by 1975. A further eighteen countries with the status of dependencies within the Commonwealth would enjoy privileged access to the Community. The existence of such a large and variegated group of countries operating their own privileged system does not fit easily into an international monetary and trading system with rules binding on all its members. Does increasing the number of countries associated with such a group increase or decrease the amount of discrimination in world trade? What steps can be taken to ease the position of the non-members

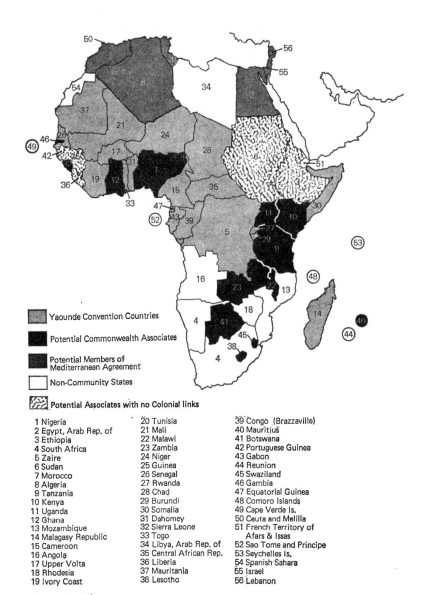

Yaounde Convention Countries

Potential Commonwealth Associates

Potential Members of
Mediterranean Agreement

Non-Community States

Potential Associates with no Colonial links

1 Nigeria	20 Tunisia	39 Congo (Brazzaville)
2 Egypt, Arab Rep. of	21 Mali	40 Mauritius
3 Ethiopia	22 Malawi	41 Botswana
4 South Africa	23 Zambia	42 Portuguese Guinea
5 Zaïre	24 Niger	43 Gabon
6 Sudan	25 Guinea	44 Reunion
7 Morocco	26 Senegal	45 Swaziland
8 Algeria	27 Rwanda	46 Gambia
9 Tanzania	28 Chad	47 Equatorial Guinea
10 Kenya	29 Burundi	48 Comoro Islands
11 Uganda	30 Somalia	49 Cape Verde Is.
12 Ghana	31 Dahomey	50 Ceuta and Melilla
13 Mozambique	32 Sierra Leone	51 French Territory of
14 Malagasy Republic	33 Togo	Afars & Issas
15 Cameroon	34 Libya, Arab Rep. of	52 Sao Tome and Principe
16 Angola	35 Central African Rep.	53 Seychelles Is.
17 Upper Volta	36 Liberia	54 Spanish Sahara
18 Rhodesia	37 Mauritania	55 Israel
19 Ivory Coast	38 Lesotho	56 Lebanon

Community Africa

and the non-associates? How far does association with the Community represent a solution to the problems of the developing countries enjoying this relationship? Does it bring nearer the realization of the demands put forward at the UNCTAD Santiago meeting for an increased voice for developing countries in the operation of the international monetary and trading systems? Does the enlargement of the Community and the association of a number of developing countries with it solve any of the problems of the Third World? Or does it create some new ones while making old problems more bearable for a limited number of countries?

These questions will be discussed under three headings. First the association of the Six with the former French and Belgian countries under the first two Yaounde Conventions; second the provision made for Commonwealth African Countries in the Treaty of Accession; and third the agreement with the Mediterranean countries.

THE SIX IN AFRICA

The Treaty of Rome provided under Article 131 for the Association with the EEC of the 'non-European countries and territories which have special relations with Belgium, France, Italy and the Netherlands'. The territories referred to under this general heading were: French West Africa, (Senegal, the Sudan, Guinea, Ivory Coast, Dahomey, Mauritania, Niger, Upper Volta), French Equatorial Africa (Middle Congo, later known as Congo Brazzaville, Ubangi-Shari, Tchad, Gaboon), St Pierre and Miquelon, the Comoro Archipelago, Madagascar and dependencies, French Somaliland, New Caledonia and dependencies, French settlements in Oceania, Southern and Antarctic territories, Togo, Belgian Congo (now Zaire), Rwanda-Urandi, Somaliland under Italian Trusteeship and Netherlands New Guinea, the Cameroons.

When the Rome Treaty was being negotiated in 1957 all these territories were still administered as colonies, so that the question of their becoming associates of the proposed European Economic Community was not a matter for their choice. Association for these colonial territories was demanded by the French on the grounds that special arrangements had to be made for their trade and economic relations. Association was in other words a necessary

34

consequence of setting up the EEC. The eighteen African countries were by far the most important of the countries to be accommodated. Even so, although covering a large part of West and Central Africa their total population was well below that of Western Germany (or Nigeria), and they included among their number some of the poorest countries in the world. Under Part IV of the Treaty of Rome the associated states benefited from the reductions of tariffs made by the Six on goods originating within the Community. At the same time they were required to reduce the duties they charged on imports from the Six, giving them in fact a 'reverse preference'. The idea was that the division of labour would thus be carried farther, the associated states would specialize in the production of those agricultural products for which their climate and geography made them particularly suitable, while the Six would specialize in producing industrial goods and farm products for which they had special advantages. This arrangement, based on good intentions, was nevertheless very one-sided. Because of the disparity in economic power and the difference in size between the Community and associate states, the advantages inevitably lay with the former. For the Six, integration meant an eventual Common Market of 180 million people. The Associated States however operated as eighteen separate markets with no arrangements for the creation of a Common Market. This process has been described as the creation of '18 captive markets in Africa'.*

Reverse Preferences

In setting up a free trade area between countries which are at a different stage of development from those of the Community members, the question of reciprocity is perhaps the most difficult to resolve. It is a characteristic of developing countries that they are trying to establish industries of their own and that these require protection. In the Yaounde Convention the idea of 'reverse preferences' was established ostensibly in order to conform to GATT rules. In practice the African countries have been able to maintain a measure of protection by imposing revenue duties. The idea that reverse preferences are a serious problem has nevertheless continued to be widely held. The question is, what can the Com-

* See P.N.C.P. Okigbo, *Africa and the Common Market*, Longmans 1967.

munity members expect by way of special treatment for their exports to the parties to an agreement of this kind?

'Reverse preferences' have been condemned by spokesmen for the developing countries at UNCTAD meetings and elsewhere. On the other hand some developing countries regard them as an essential token of independence. If the benefits are all one way, the argument goes, then agreements with the Community are not between states which can be in any way described as equal and independent. For some African states the idea of associate membership of the Community is resented as being an inferior status, and the question of 'reverse preferences' is closely related to this self-conscious attitude. In order to get over this difficulty, and because of increasing opposition within the Community to the principle of 'reverse preferences', both Sir Christopher Soames, Vice President of the Commission, and M. Deniau, then Commissioner in charge of external relations with developing countries, have stated that the Community would not claim exclusive customs concession in agreements with developing countries, and that these should have complete control over their external tariffs and be quite free to grant the same tariff reductions to other industrialized countries as to members of the Community. Furthermore they should be able to negotiate these concessions with non-Community countries such as the United States and Japan, and not grant them freely as a side effect of an agreement with the Community. This new approach to the question of 'reverse preferences' will affect the attitude of African countries in negotiating agreements with the Community.

The eighteen dependent territories obtained two main advantages from association. The first was that their exports could enter the market of the Six at preferential rates of duty compared with other developing countries in Africa. The second advantage was participation in the European Development Fund set up to finance development, expenditure on infrastructure and social security schemes.

The First Yaounde Convention

The fact that the EEC has always been an evolving phenomenon is illustrated by what happened to the Convention of Association of 1958 with the eighteen dependent territories. Nationalist movements in the African countries gathered momentum in the two years following the implementation of the Treaty of Rome. Former French and Belgian Colonies in Africa became independent states, so that a new form of arrangement appropriate to this change was required. The Treaty of Rome had not anticipated such a development. There was no way in which the eighteen African countries could opt out of the Convention of Association or change their position within it. Even if the Treaty had contained an 'escape' clause it would not have been in the interests of the African states at that time to denounce Association. All of them to a greater or less degree were in a weak economic position, and the possibility of access for their products to the Community market and participation in the Development Fund were advantages they could not easily forgo. Again, independence for most of the new states would have meant breaking off ties with France. For them close association with the Six rather than France alone was clearly an advantage. The result was that the newly independent states readily joined with the Commission in working out a new Convention.

Negotiations took place through 1961 and 1962, and an agreement was initialed at Yauonde, the capital of the Republic of the Cameroons, on 20 July 1963, to come into effect for a period of five years on 1 June 1964. This covered eighteen independent states, namely Burundi, Cameroon, Central African Republic, Tchad, Congo (Kinshasa) now Zaire, Congo (Brazzaville), Dahomey, Gabon, Upper Volta, Ivory Coast, Madagascar, Mali, Mauritania, Niger, Rwanda, Senegal, Somalia and Togo. Only Guinea of the former French territories refused to join the association. The legal basis of the Convention, which lasted for five years to 31 May 1969, was Part IV of the Treaty of Rome reinforced by the various Articles authorizing the Community to make treaties with independent states. This meant that the old basis of a 'special relationship' under the 1958 Convention no longer applied. In the negotiations the Six were anxious to avoid charges that they were simply continuing the colonial relationship under a different name. The source of the legal competence of the Community was not stated explicitly in the Yaounde Convention, but the argument on this point has been overtaken by events, so that discussion of which actions were covered by Article 136 and which by Article 238 has now become academic. The second Yaounde Convention, which continued and extended the first, was signed in 1969 to run from 1 January 1971 to 31 January 1975.

The provisions of the Yaounde Convention cover the commercial relationship between the Community and the eighteen states individually and the establishment of an institutional framework including a Council of Ministers. The trade provisions provided for the abolition of tariffs on imports and exports and of charges having an equivalent effect, the removal of quantitative restrictions on imports and introduced provisions concerning agricultural products. Some concessions were made to the pressure for lower tariff rates on tropical goods by reductions in the Common External Tariff on coffee, cocoa, tea, pineapples, pepper, cloves, vanilla and nutmeg. The United Kingdom came into this part of the negotiation, through an undertaking given in the context of the accession negotiations of 1962–3 to suspend duties on tea and tropical hardwoods. This was done by the Community and Britain from 1 January 1964 until 31 December 1965, and the period of suspension was later extended. So far as agricultural products covered by the Common Agricultural Policy were concerned, the interests of the Associated States were protected with regard to such crops as oilseeds and sugar, which were in competition with European products.

The Convention did not cover trade between the associated states themselves, but created a series of separate free trade areas. The member states come together however in the institutions provided for the implementation of the Convention. An Association Council, composed of members of the Council and of the Commission of the EEC and one member of the government of each associated state, meets at least once a year and its decisions are reached by 'mutual agreement' between the Community and Associated States. An Association Committee consisting of officials operates in the same sort of way as the Committee of Permanent Representatives of the member states of the Community. The Parliamentary Conference consists of equal numbers of members of the European Assembly and of the Parliaments of the Associated States. This meets once a year and receives a report from the Association Council on its activities. Finally there is a Court of Arbitration which adjudicates on disputes concerning the interpretation or application of the Convention. It consists of a

President appointed by the Association Council and four judges, two from the Associated States and two from the Community.

The provisions for financial and technical cooperation in the Yaounde Convention increased the amount of aid made available and widened the range of objectives for which it might be used. In all, some $800m. was sanctioned, of which $730m. went to the eighteen African states and $70m. to the still dependent overseas countries and territories and the four French overseas departments. The dependent territories, Territoires d'Outre Mer (TOM), consist of the remaining Dutch and French dependencies, associated under Part IV of the Treaty of Rome, under terms which are similar but distinct from those of the Yaounde Convention.* The overseas departments, Départements d'Outre Mer (DOM), are regarded in a legal sense as being part of France itself. They are treated as part of the EEC and their products, mostly bananas and sugar, are dealt with as internal products and benefit from the Common Agricultural Policy.† A high proportion of the funds available are in the form of grants from the European Development Fund, with the remainder in the form of 'soft loans' from the European Investment Bank.

The Second Yaounde Convention

Other provisions of the Yaounde Convention covered the right of establishment and provision of services on similar lines to those contained in the Treaty of Rome. In view of the great difference in social and economic conditions between the European countries and the associated states it is not easy to see how the latter would benefit from the right to invest in the Six or set up professional practices there. On the other hand the right of establishment in the Associated States was important to companies from Community countries other than France in ensuring that the discriminatory practices in favour of French nationals were not used against them.

In 1969 the Yaounde Convention was renewed for a period of

* The TOM are Surinam, Netherlands Antilles, French Polynesia, New Caledonia, Wallis and Fortuna, Comoro Islands, French Somaliland, St Pierre and Miquelon, and French Southern and Antarctic Territories.
† The DOM consist of Guadeloupe, Martinique, Réunion and Guiana.

six years ending on 31 January 1975. The changes in the second compared with the first Convention were that the level of aid was raised to $1,000m. ($82m. for the TOM and DOM), and that the Common External Tariff on tropical products was reduced following undertakings made at the second UNCTAD Conference at New Delhi in 1968. To compensate for this, the eighteen Associated States were given easier access for their agricultural products covered by the Common Agricultural Policy.

Franc Zone and Sterling Area

To sum up, the effect of the two Conventions has been to give free entry to goods from the eighteen and the dependent territories on all items except farm products covered by the CAP. These last however receive preference over similar products from other countries. The associated states have in return undertaken to eliminate their own tariffs on goods from the Community, while retaining the right to maintain tariffs for revenue purposes or to protect infant industries. This arrangement has given rise to a system of three-column tariffs – the standard rate, the preferential rate and the revenue duty rate. This system enables the governments concerned to opt out of giving a 'reverse preference' on goods imported from the Community, by fixing the standard duty at a low or nil rate and putting on a high revenue duty. The Yaounde Convention does not provide for free trade between the eighteen, and no significant moves to this end have been made.

Fourteen of the AASM countries are members of the Franc Zone, to which their currency, the CFA franc (Communauté Française Africaine), is aligned. The French, who have retained a large measure of responsibility for determining national monetary policies, have fixed the exchange parity of the CFA and French franc and guaranteed the external payments of Franc Zone members. This has meant that independence has not been complete and the CFA has been influenced more by what has happened to the French economy than by local conditions. The African states claim that the terms of trade have moved against them and that as most of them are in surplus the guarantee of their external balances is not of great value. In any case the French have ensured that no state remains in deficit for long by imposing penal interest rates and restricting the discount operations of the local banks of those that run into the red. Another criticism is that the four central banks of the Franc Zone, in West Africa, Central Africa, Mali and Malagasy, require French approval of their credit policies. These banks are responsible both for controlling the money supply and issuing medium-term credit, and funds are often channelled back to Paris to earn higher interest rates which, it is claimed, would be invested locally if management policy was in African hands.

Changes have begun to take place which will increase the flexibility of operation of the Franc Zone. In particular, governments are now allowed to hold a certain proportion of their foreign exchange earnings outside the Operations Account which they must maintain at the French Treasury in Paris. This will increase trade between Franc Zone and Sterling Area members by making it possible for them to set up payments unions. The main difficulties in the way of this trade are parity differences and the complexity of transferring funds between different currency systems. Trade agreements between Nigeria and Niger have until now met with little success, as they have only got as far as setting up a framework for trade without having the credit reserves needed to finance a payments union. Another much needed change in Franc Zone practice is the amendment of the regulations covering investment. What is needed here is some form of credit insurance on investments in the Franc Zone, or changes in exchange control policy to allow for dividend and capital repatriation on more attractive terms.

Extending Yaounde Convention terms to Commonwealth African states will increase the demand for faster progress towards African monetary union. This clearly presents considerable problems for states which are at very different stages of development, ranging from the very poor ones such as Chad, Niger and Malawi to Nigeria, the largest African nation. One of the benefits which European Community enlargement could bring to Africa should be to end the rigid separation of states into Franc Zone and Sterling Area and to open up the possibility of economic and commercial cooperation between all African states.

COMMONWEALTH AFRICA

The extension of the Community to include the United Kingdom meant that arrangements had to be made to cover the interests of other Commonwealth countries, in line with the principle that it was not possible to break economic links which had grown up over time, which had been recognized in the two Yaounde Conventions. These agreements, having started off as internal multilateral arrangements under the Treaty of Rome, have become an external relationship of the Community with the Associated African States and Malagasy (AASM), the name given to the association formed by the eighteen African states.

The existence of this privileged position enjoyed by the AASM has been criticized by other developing countries, particularly at the UNCTAD Conferences. The Latin American states have persistently called upon the EEC to abolish its preferential system. One of the principal critics of the Yaounde System was Dr Raoul Prebisch when Secretary General of UNCTAD. At the same time considerable political changes have been taking place in the African states and in their attitudes towards the European Community. The situation is both simplified and complicated by the fact that two main trading zones, Commonwealth and French Africa, had been established in pre-independence days. The fact that the former colonial powers had introduced the division into English- and French-speaking territories was a further problem.

The nature of the regimes introduced was also different. The Commonwealth was based on decentralization of policy on trade and finance, while the Franc Zone was firmly controlled from Paris. The building up of commercial and financial links between the former colonies and the metropolitan countries inevitably meant that the direction of trade was not greatly influenced by independence. In the 1960s there was a proliferation of organizations whose object was the promotion of African unity. They included the Organization of African Unity (OAU) and various regionally directed groups, notably the Casablanca Group, the Monrovia Group and the Entente Group. Attempts at closer economic integration took place with varying degrees of success between groups of states in East Africa and West Africa.

Arusha and Lagos Conventions

The fact that Nigeria and the three Commonwealth East African states, Kenya, Uganda and Tanzania, all applied for association and negotiated agreements with the EEC during the 1960s represented a considerable step towards ending the division between Community and Commonwealth Africa. Proposals for association which had been made to the African states as part of the arrangements for the enlargement of the Community should carry this process a stage further. Of the two existing agreements, the Arusha Convention between Kenya, Uganda and Tanzania and the EEC which came into force on 1 January 1971 is the more important. Under the Treaty and its subsequent amendments the Community granted duty-free entry to all products originating in the three East African countries, which in turn granted tariff concessions on fifty-nine products, covered by duties ranging from two to nine per cent ad valorem. In addition, products covered by the Common Agricultural Policy received more favourable treatment on entry into the EEC. The main products benefiting were coffee, pyrethrum, cassava, pineapples, cloves and certain vegetables. The East African countries were free under the treaty to establish free trade areas or customs unions amongst themselves or with third countries, but they undertook that products originating in the EEC would not be treated less favourably as the result of setting up any such trading arrangement. The Arusha Convention did not provide for aid from the European Development Fund nor for the establishment of institutions. The agreement is due to expire on 31 January 1975, the same date as the Second Yaounde Convention.

The agreement making Nigeria an associate member of the EEC was signed in Lagos on 16 July 1966. Under its provisions all Nigerian exports except groundnut oil, palm oil, cocoa beans and plywood were to enter the EEC free of duty. The four excepted products would be subject to tariff quotas. In return Nigeria undertook to grant duty-free entry to Community goods. Nigeria undertook to avoid discrimination against non-Community members by imposing fiscal duties instead of customs duties and charging these on imports from the Community. The agreement did not provide for aid from the EEC, but an Association Council was to

43

be established consisting of an EEC and a Nigerian representative meeting once a year at ministerial level, and more frequently at ambassadorial level. Because of the political situation in Nigeria the Treaty did not come into effect and expired at the end of May 1969. One interesting aspect of the Lagos Association Treaty was the fact that it was criticized by both the United Kingdom and the United States as not being in accordance with GATT rules.

The Arusha and Lagos Conventions dealt with only a small number of the Commonwealth African countries. Enlarging the Community necessitated arrangements to ensure that trade relations between Commonwealth countries and the new European Community should be safeguarded either by the establishment of association arrangements similar to those already enjoyed by the Francophone African countries or on the lines of the Arusha Agreement or by some special trading agreement. The idea was that countries which had previously had no special arrangement with the Community, such as Zambia, Ghana, Sierra Leone and The Gambia, should not be at a disadvantage compared with the participants in the Yaounde and Arusha Agreements. For purposes of convenience, the arrangements for the Commonwealth African countries will be dealt with in Chapter Three, which describes the measures affecting the Commonwealth as a whole.

MEDITERRANEAN POLICY

The countries of the Mediterranean have always been of special interest to the Community, particularly to France and Italy. The association agreements with Greece, Turkey and Spain have already been described, but these are only part of what is expected to develop into a comprehensive Mediterranean policy. In terms of geography and commerce, close relations with the countries bordering the Mediterranean are an historical fact. What is less readily acceptable is any move towards making the Mediterranean into an exclusive Community interest. The Six reached agreement on the general lines of a Mediterranean policy before the Community was enlarged. In principle it was decided in the summer of 1972 that there should be a 'single overall policy' for the enlarged Community in its industrial and agricultural trade with Malta, Cyprus, Spain, Israel, Egypt, Jordan, Lebanon, Morocco, Tunisia and Algeria, plus Greece and Turkey which were already associates. This arrangement was seen as helping to tidy up relationships between the Nine and the developing world.

The connection between the Community and Mediterranean countries ranges much wider than trade in agricultural and manufactured products. The Six obtain a large proportion of their oil from North Africa, and some four million migrant workers from the Mediterranean countries have come to the Community, particularly to West Germany and France. For these countries the Community is a principal market for their agricultural products, an outlet for their surplus labour, and a source of supply of manufactured goods. Before the negotiations for the enlargement of the Community in 1971 the Six had made a number of bilateral trade agreements on a piecemeal basis with the Mediterranean countries. These were generally limited to trade and provided for preferential treatment over a period for the products of the countries concerned. The most important of these were the association agreements with Greece and Turkey already described, and those with Tunisia, Morocco and Malta.

Existing agreements

The arrangements with the various Mediterranean countries in force at the beginning of 1973 are summarized below.

Malta. The agreement between the European Community and Malta came into force in April 1971, and provides for the establishment of a customs union in two five-year stages. In the first stage, duties on most of Malta's imports from the Community are to be reduced in three steps by up to thirty-five per cent or to the MFN level. The Community has cut its tariffs on most Maltese exports by seventy per cent, but some textile exports are subject to quotas. In the second five-year stage the Community will remove all duties on Maltese industrial products and Malta will continue to move towards the adoption of the common customs tariff.

Cyprus. Negotiations for a ten-year association agreement with Cyprus were concluded late in 1972. The Community has agreed to cut tariffs on industrial goods from Cyprus and give preferential

45

treatment to its agricultural products. The preference for exports of wine and other farm products to Britain was safeguarded under the agreement.

Tunisia and Morocco. These states have trading agreements which came into force in September 1969. The Community has abolished customs duties and quotas on industrial goods other than cork, coal and steel from both countries. There is also an eighty per cent preference for citrus fruits, subject to a proviso that they must not be sold below an agreed 'reference price', and also a reduced levy on olive oil and concessions on fish products and wheat. In return both countries have made tariff and quota reductions on certain Community goods. Neither of these agreements provides for financial aid or the free movement of labour. Both Morocco and Tunisia were formerly French overseas territories, and the object of the agreements made with the Community was to secure the trading concessions then enjoyed on a Community basis. Any extension of present agreements with these two countries will be as a part of the proposed free trade area with them and Algeria – the three Mahgreb countries.

Algeria. A first round of negotiations for an association agreement covering development aid, trade and the movement of workers was completed in mid-1972. The agreement would provide for industrial free trade between the Community and Algeria with special rules for steel, manufactured goods and petroleum products. Preferential treatment, similar to that granted to Tunisia and Morocco, would apply to farm products. The agreement, expected to come into operation in 1974, will regularize the position of Algeria in relation to the Community and end the ad hoc arrangements that have been obtained since Algeria became independent.

Israel. Trading arrangements between the Community and Israel are covered by a five-year preferential agreement dating from 1964. This provides for a gradual reduction of between ten and thirty per cent of Israel's tariffs on well over half the industrial and agricultural goods imported from the Community. Cuts of up to fifty per cent are being made on some eighty-five per cent of Community imports from Israel. Concessions on Israel's agricultural exports, including a forty per cent preference on citrus fruits, also apply.

Egypt. A preferential five-year agreement was negotiated in October 1972. Under this agreement the Community is to cut tariffs on imports of Egyptian industrial goods by stages. These will be more gradual for cars and aluminium products, and petroleum products will be subject to a special rate of reduction. Cotton fabrics will be covered by a reduced duty quota. The Community duty on citrus fruits will be cut by sixty per cent compared with forty per cent for Israel and Spain. Concessions also apply to Egyptian exports of rice and onions. In return the Egyptian tariff on Community goods will be reduced by stages. This agreement is complicated by the assertion of Egypt's right to boycott Community firms trading with Israel. General declarations banning discrimination have been exchanged, but the Egyptian government has specified that the ban can be overridden by concerns of national security.

Lebanon. The trade and technical cooperation agreement with the Lebanon has been extended pending the negotiation of a new agreement.

Yugoslavia. A trading agreement with Yugoslavia came into force in May 1970. This treaty, which contains no preferential element, was the first to be made between the Community and an East European state. It provides for MFN treatment for trade in industrial goods, while Yugoslavia receives concessions on exports of baby beef to the Community. Proposals for extending the agreement are under consideration. These would cover industrial and technical cooperation, the conditions of trade for Yugoslav agricultural products. Although geographically in the Mediterranean region Yugoslavia, as an East European state, is in a different category from the rest of the countries covered by the Mediterranean policy of the Community.

The new situation

The conclusion of the Brussels negotiations created a new situation for the Mediterranean countries. They now had to decide how far the arrangements they had made with the Six were appropriate to a Community of Nine which had concluded agreements with a wide range of countries in the Commonwealth covering the sort of agricultural products and manufactured goods which they themselves produced. At the same time the fact that Britain, Ireland and Denmark had joined the Community had greatly increased its population and changed the balance of self-sufficiency for a number of agricultural products. Furthermore the need to safeguard the interests of Britain's traditional trading partners in the Commonwealth meant that the Mediterranean countries were dealing with a Community with a different motivation from that of the Six.

At first sight, for the Community to form closer trading and commercial links with the Mediterranean countries seems to be an obvious step to take. However the problem which it raises is a very simple one, namely that it is not possible to have special arrangements with groups of developing countries in different parts of the world which are equally advantageous to all. In other words the Mediterranean policy may be in conflict with the interests of the Yaounde countries and the Commonwealth associables, as well as non-associables everywhere.

The proposals put forward by the Commission for a Mediterranean Policy are of special concern to the Mahgreb countries and to Spain and Israel. These countries together with Malta have been given priority because the Community was already committed to negotiating new agreements with them to replace others existing or superseded now. These countries are also seen as forming the basis for an overall policy which could be adopted at a later stage to cover all the Mediterranean. The proposed Mediterranean agreement would be on the basis of a free trade area between individual countries and the Community. The latter would offer complete free trade, arrived at by tariff cuts over an agreed period of years. Because of the nature of the countries concerned two specific problems arise. One of these is the treatment of refined oil products from the Mahgreb countries which at present are admitted to the Six under nil-duty tariff quotas incorporated in past agreements with Morocco and Tunisia. This arrangement does not apply to Algeria, whose trade was not covered by the agreement current at the time of the conclusion of the Brussels negotiations. The second major problem concerns the treatment for imports of sensitive products into the Community from Spain and Israel.

To conclude a Mediterranean policy will be difficult from another point of view. This is that it brings together countries which are regarded as suitable for full membership of the Community at a later stage, notably Spain, Greece and Turkey, Israel, which is in a midway position and is neither a developing country nor in Europe, and the Mahgreb countries, some of which have in the past had very close economic links with France. For example in 1958, when the Treaty of Rome was signed, Algeria was still officially part of metropolitan France. Another problem is the fact that the poorest parts of the old Community are mostly in the Mediterranean region and depend on and compete with the same products as those exported from countries of the South and East Mediterranean. The movement of industry to the Mediterranean coasts of France and Italy, as well as Spain, has raised the question of pollution. This clearly is a problem which should be dealt with on a Mediterranean scale rather than left to the attentions of individual countries.

There are therefore good reasons for initiating a Community Mediterranean policy. For Britain such a policy poses the need to adopt objective Community attitudes at a rather early stage after becoming a member. For the Community as a whole a Mediterranean policy has wider political implications, bringing it into contact, if not conflict, with the policies of the USSR and the United States. More than any other aspect of the activities of the extended Community, a Mediterranean policy demonstrates the truth of Professor Hallstein's statement that the Community is in politics, not in business.

3. The Commonwealth Adjusts to the Community

In the legal sense, the fact that Britain has joined the European Community does not affect the position of the Commonwealth countries. The Queen's constitutional position as head of State and of the Commonwealth continues as before, with Her Majesty as the link between Britain and the Commonwealth countries. Entry into the European Community requires no changes in the constitution of the Commonwealth countries or in their ties with Britain. However the fact that the Community is responsible for such important economic relationships as tariff policy and preferences, and provides a certain amount of aid through the European Development Fund, means that most Commonwealth countries must take account of the changed situation of the United Kingdom.

The Commonwealth countries divide up into no less than six broad categories in terms of their relationship with the European Community. These are:

1   The independent Commonwealth countries in Africa, the Caribbean, the Indian Ocean and the Pacific;
2   British dependent territories;
3   Gibraltar and Hong Kong;
4   India, Bangladesh, Sri Lanka, Singapore and Malaysia;
5   Mediterranean Commonwealth countries;
6   The developed Commonwealth.

Each of these separate categories has a differen. relationship with the European Community, ranging from a formal association of the Yaounde type down to the indirect impact on a part of the trade of some Commonwealth countries which British membership will entail. The modern Commonwealth consists of thirty-two independent states together with the British dependent territories. Put another way, the Commonwealth consists of four rich countries – Australia, Canada, New Zealand and the United Kingdom – and a large number of countries at different stages of development. These range in population size from India with 537 million to The Gambia with 316,000. The independent states meet together in the annual Commonwealth Prime Ministers' Conference and have numerous other contacts at official level between meetings. All the Commonwealth countries except the dependent territories have their own political lives to live and their part to play in the world economy. The independent members each have their own priorities, which may be expressed through participation in the Group of Seventy-Seven, or regional bodies like the Organization of African States, through membership of the Colombo Plan or of the OECD Development Assistance Committee. Canada's proximity to the United States and the fact that it occupies part of the same continental area as the Caribbean Commonwealth obviously affects her external policy, as does the position of Australia and New Zealand in relation to Japan and South East Asia.

While it can be argued that the impact of British membership of the European Community upon the other Commonwealth countries has been safeguarded by the arrangements made in the Treaty of Accession, this is a matter which can only be decided country by country by the impact of the new situation on trade and development. At a different level the Commonwealth countries will be affected by changes which the enlargement of the Community makes in the operation of the GATT and of the world monetary system. Moving now from the general to the particular, what are the arrangements made for the individual Commonwealth countries?

The Independent developing countries

The independent Commonwealth countries in Africa, the Caribbean, the Indian Ocean and the Pacific, were given the choice between three options. These were association under a renewed Yaounde Convention, association on the lines of the Arusha Convention, or a commercial agreement to facilitate and expand trade with the Commonwealth. The largest group of countries to which these options applied is in Africa. They are Botswana, The Gambia, Ghana, Kenya, Lesotho, Malawi, Nigeria, Sierra Leone, Swaziland, Tanzania, Uganda and Zambia. The other countries concerned are Barbados, Guyana, Jamaica, Trinidad and Tobago in the Caribbean, Fiji, Tonga and Western Samoa in the Pacific Ocean, and Mauritius in the Indian Ocean. Mauritius applied for participation in the Second Yaounde Agreement and was approved by the Council of Ministers on 21 March 1972.

These countries are offered association with the Community on the principle that they have a 'comparable economic and production structure' to the existing Yaounde Associates. As a criterion for acceptance it is clearly very widely drawn in terms of geographical size and stage of development. While African countries as diverse as Nigeria and The Gambia are acceptable the Asian Commonwealth countries, which include some of the largest and poorest of its members, are regarded by the European Community as non-associables.

Dependent territories

The dependent territories of the United Kingdom will be associated with the enlarged Community under Part IV of the Rome Treaty. The colonial territories and dependencies, which now consist of small and scattered ports and islands, many in remote parts of the world, once regarded as valuable strategic military bases or trading posts, are still the responsibility of the British government. Hong Kong, with a population of nearly four million, is an exception in being treated as a dependency largely on political grounds. The territories covered in the Treaty of Accession are: Bahamas*, Bermuda, British Antarctic Territory, British Indian Ocean Territory, British Solomon Island Protectorate, British Virgin Islands, Brunei, Cayman Islands, Central and Southern Line Islands, Falkland Islands and Dependencies, Gilbert and Ellis Islands Colony, Montserrat, New Hebrides (with France), Pitcairn, St Helena and Dependencees (Ascension and Tristan da Cunha), Seychelles, Turks and Caicos Islands, West Indian Associates States (Antigua, Domenica, Grenada, St Lucia, St Vincent, St Kitts, Nevis and Anguilla).

* The Bahamas became independent on 10 July 1973.

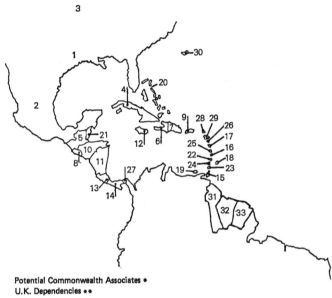

Potential Commonwealth Associates *
U.K. Dependencies **
E.C. Associates ***

1 United States
2 Mexico
3 Canada
4 Cuba
5 Guatemala
6 Haiti
7 Dominican Republic
8 El Salvador
9 Puerto Rico
10 Honduras
11 Nicaragua
12 Jamaica *

13 Costa Rica
14 Panama
15 Trinidad and Tobago *
16 Martinique***
17 Guadeloupe***
18 Barbados *
19 Netherlands Antilles***
20 Bahama Islands *
21 Belize **
22 St. Lucia **
23 Grenada **
24 St. Vincent **

25 Dominica
26 Antigua **
27 Canal Zone
28 Virgin Islands (U.S.)
29 St. Kitts-Nevis-
    Anguilla **
30 Bermuda**
31 Guyana *
32 Surinam***
33 French Guiana***

Community links with Caribbean

The arrangements governing the association with the Overseas Countries and Territories of the Community expire on 31 January 1975 and a comprehensive arrangement will be worked out to apply to all dependent countries from that date.

Hong Kong and Gibraltar

The provisions of the Paris and Rome Treaties will not be applicable to Hong Kong, which because of the size of its population and its political situation is not regarded as suitable for inclusion among the dependent territories. It has been agreed that Hong Kong will be included in the Generalized Preference Scheme of the enlarged Community.

Gibraltar will be covered by Article 227 of the Rome Treaty, which states that the provisions of the Treaty should apply to any European Territory for whose external relations a member state is responsible. As Gibraltar is not a part of the United Kingdom customs territory, it has been agreed, at the request of Gibraltar, that it should not be included in the customs territory of the enlarged Community.

The non-associables

The fact that the Commonwealth is a worldwide grouping of independent states and dependencies makes it extremely difficult to associate all its members with a regional body such as the European Community. Whatever exceptions are made inevitably create problems and hardships. This is particularly so with the independent developing countries of the Commonwealth, in Asia, the Far East and Oceania. The main countries concerned are India, Bangladesh, Sri Lanka, Malaysia and Singapore. For these countries the Treaty of Accession does no more than state that trade problems including the question of Indian exports of sugar to the Community will be examined after the enlargement of the Community and that the countries concerned would benefit from the Generalized Preference Scheme. The Community tariff on tea will continue to be suspended, to the considerable benefit of India and Sri Lanka.

Malta and Cyprus

At the time of the negotiations Malta already had an association agreement with the Community offering preferential trading arrangements, but not aid. Cyprus concluded an agreement early in 1973. These agreements are described elsewhere (pages 45–6).

THE MEMBERSHIP CATALOGUE

Simply to catalogue Commonwealth countries according to the arrangement offered to them under the Treaty of Accession does not give any very clear idea of what the effects of these changes will be. At this stage these can only be indicated in terms of possible gains and losses. Looking at the new Community line-up, how are these likely to be distributed? The principal gainers will obviously be the Six, who secure considerably improved access to the British market and an annual contribution of some £500m. from Britain in support of the Common Agricultural Policy. The associable independent Commonwealth countries should stand to benefit from easier access to the enlarged Community but this would depend on the actual range of products they had to offer. The same advantages would apply to the Yaounde countries which obtained preferential access to the United Kingdom market. At the same time it could be argued that the more countries have preferential and special trading arrangements with the Community the less valuable these advantages are. The prospect of a reduction in the tariffs on manufactured goods in the GATT would also mean an erosion of preferences. This is another aspect of the general question as to whether the enlargement of the Community, and the increase in the number of states associated with it in one form or another, competes with or complements the global arrangements for organizing trade and currency within the world economy.

But in all cases where an attempt is made to assess the importance of a new institution it is necessary to look back and consider what things were like before it was set up. Would the reduction of trade barriers and the creation of preferences on the exports of the developing countries have gone farther if the Rome Treaty had never been signed, and the European states had all gone their separate ways? The only possible answer to this is the general comment that the tariff structure of the Community today is much more liberal and outward-looking than the structure of the national tariffs of the Six in the late 1950s. One aspect of this is the fact that the trade of the Six including France with developing countries not associated with the Community has increased more rapidly than that with the Francophone countries. Having said that, it is necessary to remember that even if the Rome Treaty had not been signed the world would not have stood still. The movement towards independence for the African states would have gone forward, some kind of economic and political cooperation would have evolved in Western Europe, possibly in the OECD or NATO, and the global institutions would have been faced with the same problems, particularly in the relationship between the rich and poor countries of the world.

For the developing countries of the Commonwealth the enlargement of the Community and the changes it brings in their relationship with Britain raise one major question. Will Community policies be more, or less, protectionist towards them because of the accession of Britain? Here also the subject is complicated because the trading patterns of many countries, including the developing countries, were in many cases changing. The major problems centre around the Common Agricultural Policy of the Community where the relationship of a particular country with the Community can determine the extent of its trade in a major product. This applies particularly to sugar, vegetable oils and oilseeds, rice, fruit and vegetables, cereals, maize and tobacco.

COMMONWEALTH PREFERENCE

When the GATT Agreement was formulated in the late 1940s member countries were allowed to retain their existing preference systems in relation to dependent territories or countries with longstanding political associations. The two most important exceptions to the GATT non-discrimination rule under this heading were Commonwealth Preference and the arrangements made by France for her overseas territories. The Commonwealth preference system had operated since the early 1930s and together with the organization of the Sterling Area had provided the framework within which the trade of the United Kingdom and the Commonwealth countries was carried on. Until late in the 1950s the fact that the Commonwealth Preference Scheme would have to be abandoned if Britain joined the European Economic Community was still regarded as a major reason why this could never take place. At the time of the 1962–3 negotiations for UK entry, much of the argument was in terms of Commonwealth or Common Market, as if the two were alternatives. Since that time the composition and character of the Commonwealth has changed considerably. The emergence of independent states in Asia and Africa and the Caribbean alongside the members of the 'old Commonwealth', Australia, New Zealand, Canada, has introduced a new form of association. Formerly Britain was able to turn her back on Europe and face outwards to the deep blue sea and the distant countries of the Commonwealth. Today she is one of thirty-two independent Commonwealth countries. While the importance of Britain within the Commonwealth has declined that of some of its member states has greatly increased.

Canada, Australia and to a less extent New Zealand, from being historically British countries by population and tradition, have now developed interests and external policies which are peculiarly their own. While the Commonwealth continues to exist and is evolving new and significant relationships between its members it is no longer the focus of their economic and political life as it once was. The member countries do not turn automatically to Britain as the principal market for their products and major source of supplies and capital. The preference system had the effect, which the Second World War continued, of creating close economic ties between members which lasted effectively from 1932 to the early 1950s. In 1952 some forty per cent of British exports went to the Commonwealth, by 1972 this figure had fallen to about twenty per cent.

The erosion of Commonwealth Preference was due to a number of factors. One was the emergence of the newly independent countries, most of which did not grant preference in their markets to the United Kingdom although Britain continued to grant it to them for foodstuffs and raw materials, and to a less extent for manufactured products. Another factor was the creation of EFTA, whose industrial products received treatment at least as favourable as those from the Commonwealth countries. The value of a preference

57

depends on the size of the full rate of duty on the products concerned. The Kennedy Round introduced wide-ranging reductions in tariffs on manufactures, effective by January 1972. These reductions affected the rates of duty of the UK tariff, and therefore the level of Commonwealth Preference, on such items as textiles, tobacco, clothing and footwear, and spices.

The running down of the Commonwealth Preference Scheme was taking place at the same time as the developing countries of the world were looking for ways and means of putting forward their views on major world problems. The creation of UNCTAD in 1964 was a major step in making this possible. Its main object is to promote international trade with a view to accelerating economic development. It is also concerned with the formulation of new principles and policies for trade, and is a centre for harmonizing government policies and coordinating their actions. At the first UNCTAD Conference in 1964 in Geneva, and again at the second conference in New Delhi in 1968, the whole question of preferences as a means of dealing with the exports of the developing countries was discussed. Negotiations for a scheme of generalized non-reciprocal tariffs then began to be carried on in the OECD. In May 1970 it was agreed that the member countries of the OECD could offer separate schemes of preferences to all developing countries. As a result schemes have been drawn up by the European Economic Community, the United Kingdom, the United States and other countries. The EEC scheme came into operation in 1971, the British scheme in 1972, while the United States proposals and those of Japan have still to be implemented. The countries actually granting preferences to the developing countries are Denmark, Ireland, Norway, Finland, New Zealand, Sweden, Switzerland and Austria. Australia has had its own system of preferences for developing countries since 1964.

THE MONETARY QUESTION

The discussion of the effect on the Commonwealth of the enlargement of the European Community must take account of its monetary arrangements. Strictly speaking, the UK commitment on this subject goes no farther than agreement to join in a common monetary policy as agreed at the Paris summit meeting in October

1972. In practice the period before joining saw the start of the run-down of Britain's responsibility to maintain the Sterling Area system in operation. What was this system, and what is the effect on Commonwealth countries of phasing it out?

The Sterling Area

The creation of the Sterling Area in 1931, followed by the introduction of Commonwealth Preference, was a step towards creating a stable system of trade and payments centred on the United Kingdom. It was however a partial solution affecting only the countries of the Commonwealth (except Canada) plus a number of Middle Eastern states and the Irish Republic, which were drawn in by the dictates of economic policy. The Sterling Area members agreed to peg their currencies to sterling, so that they had in effect a joint currency no matter what its national name might be. This state of affairs continued through the 1930s with sterling floating against the rest of the world. The outbreak of the Second World War necessitated some more formal arrangements than the gentlemen's agreements which had operated effectively up to then. The result was a system under which the 'Scheduled Territories', as the Sterling Area countries were called, were exempted from the exchange controls imposed on third countries. They in turn pegged their currencies to sterling, held their reserves in London in sterling, and introduced controls to prevent funds leaking out to third countries.

The beginning of the long period of difficulty for sterling as an international currency was the accumulation of vast liquid debts during the war period. These sterling balances, as they were called, had reached the sum of £3,500m. by 1945, against which Britain held reserves of about £1,000m. The setting up of the International Monetary Fund in 1945, with its various mechanisms for supporting the currencies of member countries, raised the dollar to the position of the world's major reserve currency, with sterling in a subordinate role but nevertheless subject to speculative pressures. The establishment of GATT with its non-discrimination rule prevented any extension of the Commonwealth Preference System and indirectly led to the creation of the European Economic Community and EFTA, as permitted exceptions to the GATT rules.

59

On the political front, the coming of independence to so many Commonwealth countries meant a complete change from the historical relationships of the 1930s and earlier between Britain and the rest of the Commonwealth. Australia and to a less extent New Zealand were followed by India and the African and Caribbean states in looking for outlets for their products other than the British market. In the United Kingdom the immediate post-war period was one of extreme difficulty, with recurring balance of payments problems superimposed on all the frustrations involved in the redeployment of the national resources in terms of products and markets. By the mid-1950s British industry was already beginning to look on the West European and American markets as areas of faster growth demanding more sophisticated and technologically advanced products than the Commonwealth. Even so it was not until 1968 that UK exports to Western Europe attained a value greater than those to the Commonwealth.

Holding the rate

From the mid 1950s onwards, Britain was involved in one balance of payments crisis after another. Explanation of the reasons for this situation and suggestions on what should have been done about it preoccupied economists and commentators to the exclusion of more positive questions such as how to keep the rate of inflation under control. Under the IMF system, national currencies were given an official rate of exchange expressed in terms of US dollars and gold. For practical purposes what mattered was the exchange rate against the dollar, and the national authorities intervened in the foreign exchange market to keep this within defined limits. Under the IMF rules, changes in exchange rates were expected to be few and far between and to be made with the object of curing 'fundamental disequilibria'. The efforts of the Labour government to maintain the exchange rate led to drastic deflation of the economy and a continuing fall in industrial investment. Restrictions on foreign investment and on the use of sterling to finance international trade caused the City to look for alternatives and led to the development of the Euro-dollar market. At the same time members of the Overseas Sterling Area (OSA), alarmed at the weakness of sterling, began to diversify their reserves. This was a manoeuvre which could not be pressed to its final conclusion as the wherewithal to convert this amount of sterling by allowing long-term capital conversion did not exist in the Sterling Area. Up to 1969 the Sterling Area received about half Britain's direct overseas investment, but the percentage fell to thirty-five per cent in 1970. However this fall was offset to some extent by large portfolio investment in Australia.

Devaluation

The turning point in the fortunes of sterling was the devaluation of November 1967. Up to then the reserve function of sterling had been cited as a compelling reason for maintaining the IMF exchange rate. The fact that no compensation was paid to the central banks of member countries which suffered a loss in dollar terms through devaluation underlined the weakness of the Sterling Area and increased the need for its members to seek an alternative. The Basle Agreement of 1968, to which the European and American governments were parties, slowed down the flight from sterling by giving a dollar value guarantee against any further devaluation of the pound to countries agreeing to keep a fixed proportion of their reserves in sterling.

Two further developments in the international monetary field have speeded the end of the Sterling Area. The first was the decision of the British government to join the European Community, which necessarily involved running down the reserve currency role of sterling and eventual participation in a European monetary union. The other change, or rather series of changes, was set off by President Nixon's new economic policy of 15 August 1971, which led to the effective devaluation of the dollar and to the introduction of new dollar parities at the Smithsonian Agreement in December 1971 and a further devaluation in February 1973. One of the results of these activities was the floating of the pound.

The Floating Pound

Among the factors which made it impossible to hold the rate of 2.60 dollars to the pound were loss of confidence abroad in Mr

Heath's government's ability to check inflation, Mr Barber's 1972 budget statement that he would not defend an unrealistic exchange rate by sacrificing expansion, and continuing labour problems in spite of the existence of the new Industrial Relations Act. All these things were mixed up in the sterling crisis which began about 16 June 1972 and led to the floating of the pound a week later. In between, the Bank of England gave very substantial support to sterling, as did the central banks of the Six which, under the Common Market currency agreement which Britain had joined on 1 May, were pledged to keep fluctuations of members' currencies within rather narrow limits.

The operation of the Sterling Area was brought to an end when British and Commonwealth capital formerly free to move without restriction in the rest of what was the Sterling Area became subject to exchange control. The exchange control regulations now applied to the OSA differ from those applied to the External Account Area (EAA) and are, on the whole, considerably less restrictive than the latter. The major change in the treatment of the OSA lies in the requirement to obtain permission to carry out transactions with the OSA territories, rather than in the limits imposed on such transactions. Thus bona fide direct investment in the OSA is not subject to restriction, and foreign exchange for this purpose can be obtained at the official rate. In contrast, foreign exchange for direct investment in the EAA has to be borrowed abroad, bought through the investment currency pool at a premium, and only in special cases may it be acquired from the Bank of England. And although personal capital movements to the OSA are now subject to an upper limit, this is well in excess of that applied to the EAA. The only members of the Overseas Sterling Area now are Britain, the Isle of Man, the Channel Islands and the Irish Republic.

The approach of EEC membership on 1 January 1973 made it necessary for the UK government to implement its pledge to introduce 'a progressive alignment of the external characteristics of sterling' with those of the other Community countries. This meant that the preferential treatment on exchange controls, the access to the London capital market, and the reserve function of sterling which members of the Sterling Area previously enjoyed, had to be phased out. Floating the pound simply brought some of the consequent measures forward. In the long run the ending of the Sterling Area should strengthen the British economy through the reduction of the burden of overseas commitments, but lasting benefits will depend to a large extent on the reform of the international monetary system.

4. Old Commonwealth and New Community

At the time of the Macmillan government's attempt to negotiate entry into the EEC, many people regarded Britain as facing the choice between Europe and the Commonwealth. In doing so, those of an older generation at least were thinking principally of relationships with what had until quite recently been called the White Dominions. Before the Second World War the Commonwealth had served an important function in keeping these countries – Canada, Australia, New Zealand and South Africa – in touch with British foreign policy, in whose formation the resources and interests of the Dominions played an important part. This aspect of Commonwealth activity began to lose its significance in the late 1940s when it became clear that Britain's position in the world depended upon the Atlantic alliance and the nuclear deterrent, whether in American or British hands.

The change in the British situation, accompanied by the coming of independence to the developing countries of the Commonwealth, meant that a new form of relationship with the Dominions had to be found. Through the 1950s and 60s the new Commonwealth was gradually evolved. This has been a slow and steady process, which it must be said has not had any wide appeal to the British public at large. Some have seen the Commonwealth as a means of reconciling the racial antipathies between the developing and industrialized countries and have therefore emphasized its multi-racial character. Another view, tinged by nostalgia, looked back to the great-power days of British history and found difficulty in adapting to the new situation in the Commonwealth. The nature of the Commonwealth as a grouping of independent countries which cuts across a whole host of other alliances of all kinds has tended to emphasize its weakness and obscure the very useful functions which it does perform. The Commonwealth has never had any kind of constitution and it was not until the meeting of the Heads of Government in Singapore in 1971 that a Declaration of Commonwealth Principles was drawn up and given unanimous approval. This document spelt out some of the more important principles shared by Heads of Government and declared that it was the intention that these should be fostered and extended. The full text of the Declaration is given in Appendix 3.

COMMONWEALTH OR REGIONAL COOPERATION

The developed countries of the Commonwealth, Australia, Canada and New Zealand, are all affected by British membership of the European Community. Unlike the associables however there is no specific place for them in the external arrangements of the Community. New Zealand, because of its dependence on the British market, has been able to negotiate special measures which are described below (pages 70–71). The impact of enlarging the Community will be felt by the developed Commonwealth in two different ways. The first will be the direct effects on their trade with Britain and the European Community. The second, arising from this, will involve the change in direction of their own external relationships as a result of Community enlargement. This could mean that Canadian dependence on the American economy will increase and that Australia and New Zealand would concentrate increasingly on building up trade in South East Asia. Both these developments were in motion before the enlargement of the Community took place.

The question is, whether a move towards major regional groupings on a Continental basis will help the development of the world economy. In his Third Report,* Mr Arnold Smith, Secretary-General of the Commonwealth Secretariat, warned that, 'Continental isolationism could prove as dangerous in the 1970s and 1980s as national isolationism proved in the 1920s and 1930s'. The supposed choice facing Britain between Commonwealth and Community membership is turned in a different direction for the

* *Third Report of the Commonwealth Secretary-General November 1968–November 1970*, Commonwealth Secretariat, Marlborough House, London.

developed Commonwealth countries. For them the question is whether Commonwealth cooperation and regional cooperation are alternatives. The answer here is that the Commonwealth is only one aspect of the external relationships of these countries. Membership of the international institutions, the IMF, GATT, and the various United Nations bodies, and of the OECD and the Group of Ten at developed country level, will represent their major contribution to the development of the world economy.

How far the Commonwealth connection will continue to be a valuable relationship will depend on the use that Commonwealth countries make of it. Mr Arnold Smith also stated in his Third Report that the Commonwealth, 'should develop the two functions it performs best: promoting consultation among its members and fostering cooperation in practical fields.' In other words the work of a trans-regional association such as the Commonwealth could complement regional cooperation and prevent it becoming inward-looking and over-protectionist. If the Commonwealth can serve as a means of broadening horizons and balancing regional cooperation with wider links then it has an important function to perform in a world in which the European Community has spread its influence so widely.

The impact of British membership of the Community on the developed countries of the Commonwealth is important because of the role that they are now beginning to play in world affairs. While the importance of Britain within the Commonwealth has declined, theirs has greatly increased. Canada has become an important world power. Australia and New Zealand, from being historically British countries by population and tradition, have now developed interests in South East Asia, and post-war immigration has greatly broadened the area from which their population has been drawn. All three are affected by the reorientation of the trade of the United Kingdom. New Zealand is the most affected and special arrangements have been made covering those items produced mainly for the British market. Canada and Australia also find themselves, but to a lesser extent, in a changed situation.

THE CANADIAN POSITION

In the 1963 negotiations for British entry to the European Community there was considerable outcry about the damage likely to be inflicted on Canadian exports of manufactured goods, foodstuffs and raw materials. The reaction of Canadian business to the 1971 negotiations was by contrast remarkably unemotional and relaxed. Concern over the further erosion of commercial ties with Britain had been tempered by the realization that anything that strengthened British economic growth was likely to be in Canada's long-term interest. One reason for this admirably objective approach was the fact that whereas in 1960 one sixth of Canada's exports went to Britain, the proportion had dropped over the decade to below one eleventh. In the meantime exports to the United States, helped by the Automotive Trade Agreement, had greatly increased, and Japan had moved up to challenge Britain for the position of Canada's second largest trading partner.

In spite of these changes in the general situation, enlargement of the Community will nevertheless affect Canadian trade. Special arrangements of the kind negotiated for New Zealand and the developing Commonwealth countries would clearly have been inappropriate for Canada or Australia. For them the Common External Tariff will be applied to their industrial exports to the United Kingdom gradually over the transitional period to mid-1977, and their exports of agricultural produce will also be affected by the operation of the CAP. However, they both stand to benefit from the agreement on tariffs on some industrial materials arrived at in the Treaty of Accession. This means that from 1 January 1973 onwards, part of Canada's exports to Britain enjoy progressively less favourable terms in the UK market as the Common External Tariff and the CAP come into operation and Commonwealth Preference is phased out. At the same time the other Community members will improve their competitive position compared with Canada in the British market.

However the picture is not entirely one of increasing disadvantage. Some forty-five per cent of Canadian exports to Britain will continue to come in either duty-free under the Common External Tariff or under special terms of access negotiated for products listed in Annex B of the White Paper (Cmnd. 4715). The most significant of these for Canada are wood-pulp, newsprint, plywood, phosphorus, lead bullion, alumina, ferro-silicon, refined lead, zinc and aluminium. Of the items to which the levy will be applied under the CAP, some eight per cent consist of products such as the famous Canadian hard wheat, for which no substitute is available in the Community. All told some fifty-five per cent of Canadian exports will continue to enter the UK market either duty-free or at a rate no higher than that obtaining before 1 January 1973.

Apart from this, Canada also stands to benefit from two other possible developments in the enlarged Community. The first of these is the expectation that membership will stimulate the growth-rate of the British economy, so that Canadian exports will benefit accordingly. The second is that the commercial 'presence' of Canada in the UK will serve as a springboard to expand its business activities generally in the other Community countries. A third factor affecting Anglo-Canadian trade will be the decision taken regarding the level of tariffs between industrial countries in the GATT negotiations. So far as trade with Britain is concerned, Canada will be on a non-preferential basis, facing problems in relation to manufactured goods and agricultural products.

THE NEW ZEALAND POSITION

Unlike Canada and Australia, New Zealand was heavily involved in the negotiations for the enlargement of the European Community. All the participants in the negotiations recognized the special position of New Zealand arising from its long-established place as a major supplier of foodstuffs to the British market. Successive British governments had given assurances that New Zealand's vital interests would be protected in the negotiations. In the event, special arrangements were made to give continuing access for New Zealand exports of butter and cheese, while the position of exports of lamb was regarded as satisfactory without further action. The difficulty with agreements of this kind is that markets are not static and that developments elsewhere may very well upset what has been agreed upon in good faith. Certainly the quantities of butter to be imported into Britain in competition with what comes in under CAP would be very difficult indeed to forecast. By the end of the transitional period it should be possible to see more clearly how the CAP has developed. In the meantime the need for special arrangements for New Zealand can be explained, the nature of those negotiated summarized, and comments made on their adequacy.

The changes taking place in Commonwealth relationships were underlined for New Zealand, as for Australia and Canada, at the time of the 1962–3 negotiations for British membership of the European Community. Since then New Zealand has been taking steps to diversify her economy. Earnings of foreign exchange from exports of manufactured goods and from tourism and other services have increased considerably. Even so, farm products remain the basis of the economy and earn some eighty to eighty-five per cent of the country's export income. If New Zealand is to build up industry, it will be on the basis of imported technology, equipment, raw materials, energy and capital. For the foreseeable future, therefore, maintenance and expansion of exports of farm products will continue to be a basic objective of New Zealand policy. In the European countries improvements in agricultural productivity have been accompanied by the movement of labour into industry with a consequent increase in the gross national product. In New Zealand agriculture has already reached a very high level of productivity and transfers of labour to other sectors can only be envisaged on a very small scale. New Zealand is therefore in a unique position. Its economy, like those of many developing countries, is dependent on agriculture, with the difference that here it is sufficiently efficient to give the population a high standard of living.

The percentage of New Zealand exports going to Britain fell from about fifty-six per cent in 1958 to about thirty-nine per cent in 1969. This change reflects the very considerable efforts that have been made to diversify the range of export products and markets. However, Britain is still the principal market for butter, cheese and lamb. In 1969 about ninety per cent of New Zealand's butter, eighty per cent of its cheese, and about ninety per cent of its lamb continued to find outlets in the British market. During this time very little progress has been made in attempts to negotiate improved conditions of access for agricultural products through the GATT and elsewhere. The situation has continued therefore in which the British consumer has had in New Zealand an assured source of reasonably priced food, while British manufacturers have enjoyed preference on the sale of their goods in the New Zealand market, with considerable earnings from shipping, insurance and other services related to the trade between the two countries. At the same time it can be argued that this arrangement has enabled the people of New Zealand to build up one of the highest standards of living in the world. It is nevertheless difficult when one of the parties to the agreement decides, for perfectly adequate reasons, to move in a different direction so that all the adjustments and adaptations made by New Zealand to serve the British market are in effect no longer required.

The Special Arrangements for New Zealand

The negotiations recognized that New Zealand was the most affected of the developed countries by British membership of the European Community, and special arrangements were therefore made covering those items produced principally for the British market. The most important arrangements are those which guarantee a market for agreed quantities of New Zealand dairy products. These quantities will be reduced by successive stages over the first five years. For cheese the guaranteed quantities will be reduced by steps of ninety, eighty, sixty and forty per cent in the first four years so that they stand at twenty per cent of the initial level by the fifth year. For butter the guaranteed quantity for the first five years will be reduced by four per cent a year, so that in the fifth year exports to the United Kingdom will be at least eighty per cent of their level at the time of the negotiations of the Treaty of Accession. The quantities of butter involved were 165,811 tons in 1973 and 138,576 tons in 1977. For cheese the quantities were 68,580 tons in 1973 and 15,240 tons in 1977. The effect of these guarantees is that in terms of milk equivalent, New Zealand will be selling at least seventy-one per cent of the 1973 quantity in 1977, and this at prices guaranteed at a level based on the average of sales in the UK in the years 1969 to 1972.

The White Paper (Cmnd. 4715) points out that these guarantees are for minimum quantities and argues that New Zealand may have the prospect of selling more of these products under normal Community arrangements, particularly in the case of cheese. It also points out that the price guaranteed will be substantially above the level of recent years, so that over the five-year transition period total export earnings in the UK market, even at reduced quantities, would be 'at or above the level of those which it has enjoyed in recent years'. While this may be the case, the Commission is empowered to review the butter situation in 1975, the third year of British membership, in the light of the trading position and trends in the major producing and consuming countries of the world. This review will form the basis for decisions on arrangements to be made for butter beyond 1977. Past experience of the failure of the Commission to control the quantities of butter produced under the CAP do not inspire confidence regarding what may happen in the future.

For cheese there will be no guarantee after 1977, but as New Zealand cheese is not in competition with Community products, sales to the United Kingdom are not expected to fall. The sort of arrangements made for the future will depend on whether an effective world agreement on milk products is concluded. Another factor will be the success or otherwise of New Zealand's efforts to diversify its economy so as to reduce the dependence on exports of milk products. New Zealand lamb is in a different situation, as it is not covered by a common organization in the Community. A duty of twenty per cent is payable on mutton and lamb under the Common External Tariff, and it has been agreed that this will apply in stages to imports from New Zealand during the transitional period. The White Paper states that both Britain and New Zealand consider that 'an acceptable volume of trade in New Zealand lamb will continue to flow over such a tariff.'

Which Way for New Zealand?

These arrangements have been described as 'rather better than was at first thought likely.' Certainly they give the dairy farmers who are most affected a breathing space during which prices and quantities will be at agreed levels. However the character of these arrangements and the nature of the New Zealand economy make it inevitable that requests for special treatment will continue. In the new situation New Zealand can be expected to make every effort to reduce her dependence on the British market for her dairy produce. Exports of lamb are likely to continue, as there is no alternative source of supplies from the Community. However the Common Agricultural Policy is only one part of the international arrangements for the control of agriculture. The New Zealand government will undoubtedly lose no opportunity of pressing for the world commodity agreement covering dairy produce which was promised in the negotiations.

A further point is that the Community countries promised not to sell surplus dairy produce in markets which New Zealand must develop if she is to dispose of the quantities of butter and cheese that would otherwise have gone to Britain. This is an aspect of the situation which will no doubt be raised at meetings of Commonwealth Heads of Government and future GATT negotiations by New Zealand. In this context it must be remembered that both in the Community and Commonwealth Britain is only one member amongst a number. In the Community she is one of nine, in the Commonwealth one of thirty-two independent states. While there is no doubt that the New Zealanders are willing and anxious to solve the problems involved in coming to terms with their own regional environment, the fact that there are only 2.8 million of them makes the task ahead a formidable one.

Britain's entry into the European Community has come at a time when New Zealand is becoming involved in the affairs of Asian regional groupings, not only with the Commonwealth states of the Pacific, but also in building up trade with Japan and strengthening ties with Australia. In creating these new arrangements it is important that New Zealand should be able to sustain a continuing trade with Britain and the rest of the Community. Otherwise she will not have the economic strength and resources to take on new commitments. The case of New Zealand raises the problems of Britain's membership of the Community in their most acute form. Although the argument that the Community is an alternative to the Commonwealth is no longer regarded as valid, the continuing relationship of Britain to the Commonwealth still has importance for a number of its members.

New Zealand's problem is not just a matter of how many tons of butter and cheese can be sold to Britain. It concerns the relationship which has been built up over the years between New Zealand, Britain and the Commonwealth countries, particularly in the Pacific and South East Asia. If the Commonwealth had never existed New Zealand would not have any particular interest in Malaysia and Singapore, or be attempting at this time to assist in the development of the new states of Fiji, Western Samoa and Tonga. While the Commonwealth as a strategic and defence mechanism has ceased to exist it can still exert influence in the international institutions which now seek to organize and regulate the operation of the world economy. No country can turn its back on its own history, and it is the possibility that this might be attempted that worries so many people about British membership of the Community. The lesson which is underlined by the case of New Zealand is that the real problem posed by British entry into the Community is one of keeping a balance between the past and the future.

AUSTRALIA AND THE COMMUNITY

The position of Australia is very different from that of New Zealand. In the past decade Australia has moved away from dependence on trade with Britain and emerged as a major international trading nation. Although a dramatic change has taken place in the composition of Australia's exports, with increasing contributions from the mining and manufacturing sectors, farm products are still the major export earners. However, the level of dependence has changed considerably. In the 1940s over ninety per cent of export earnings came from agricultural products, compared with only fifty per cent in 1973. Exports of minerals which provided only four per cent of total exports in 1950–51 had reached twenty-six per cent in 1970–71. In the same period, manufactured goods increased their contribution to Australian export income from three to nineteen per cent. It is now estimated that half the Australian population depend either directly or indirectly on manufacturing industries for their livelihood. Here the principal increases have been in the export of chemicals, vehicles and spare parts, iron and steel, and machinery. Another change has been in the direction of exports. Over one third of Australia's total trade is now with Asian countries. Japan has become Australia's principal customer and one of her major suppliers.

However Europe still remains the most important single trading area for Australia. More than forty per cent of Australia's imports come from Europe and twenty-seven per cent of exports go there. Within the changed situation, Britain is no longer the major market for Australian goods but is still the principal buyer of farm products. Some eighty-three per cent of butter exports, sixty-five per cent of canned fruit, thirty-nine per cent of dried fruit, and twenty per cent of sugar exports from Australia have been absorbed by the British market during the 1960s and 1970s. It is this dependence on Britain as a market for agricultural exports that is the principal cause of concern regarding British membership of the European Community.

In the negotiations for the enlargement of the Community it was recognized by both Australia and Britain that special arrangements of the kind negotiated for New Zealand and the developing countries would be inappropriate in the case of Australia. The Common External Tariff will be applied to the industrial imports of the United Kingdom over the transitional period while Australia's exports of agricultural products will be affected by the CAP. The White Paper stated that at most only $7\frac{1}{2}$ per cent of Australian export trade would be placed at risk because of Britain's entry into the Community. In 1969–70 the United Kingdom took only twelve per cent of Australia's total exports, a very different situation from that obtaining in 1960, when Britain was still buying more than twenty-five per cent of the Australian total. If the items affected are taken as a percentage of Australia's total exports they do not appear to be very considerable. However as these items are all from the agricultural sector the impact on particular products will be considerable in some cases. The items principally affected are butter, dried, fresh and canned fruit, and meat, sugar and wheat.

The problem posed by the closing of one market is to find alternative outlets. In the case of butter the United Kingdom has been the world's largest butter importer and with the threat of continuing expansion of production in the Community it is difficult to see where countries like Australia can dispose of their output. However there are opportunities for changes within the support arrangements given to the Australian dairy industry which could change its pattern and scale. It could be that a lower level of support would put an end to subsidized marginal production so that consumers in Australia would be better off and resources could be switched to other activities. While dairy products, sugar, fruit and wheat will be affected in the British market, well over one third of

74

Australian exports to Britain consist of products which will enter duty-free or will benefit from the duty-free quotas agreed during the negotiations. Most importantly there will be no duty on raw wool, which accounts for ten per cent of UK imports from Australia. Similarly there is no duty on metalliferous ores or copper, which account for 6.4 and 2.7 per cent respectively of imports.

On balance however the possibilities are that the enlargement of the Community will present Australia with gains which will offset possible losses on agricultural exports. The most important factor, although its effect will be gradual and it is impossible to forecast its extent, is the expectation that an enlarged Community will exert a growing demand for many Australian products, especially wool, metals, meat and manufactures. If living standards continue to expand and the worst excesses of the CAP are curbed, the Community may even continue to buy some Australian dairy produce, sugar and fruit. At the same time it must be remembered that British entry into the Common Market involves ending the system of Commonwealth Preference in which Australia shared. While Australia stands to lose its old position in the British market for agricultural products, the preferences granted on British manufactures in Australia will also come to an end. This amounted to a preference margin from $7\frac{1}{2}$ to ten per cent, and according to Australian claims affected eighty-three per cent of imports from Britain.

A number of possibilities are open to Australia with regard to Commonwealth Preference. The most obvious, and therefore least likely, action would be simply to revoke Commonwealth Preference on British goods, so that they entered on the same terms as those of other countries. There are three other possibilities. One would be to retain the two-tier system of tariffs and hold out its abolition as a possible move in return for concessions from Australia's principal trading partners, Japan, the USA and the European Community. The second would be to abolish the two-tier system and fix the new rates at the level of the old British preferential rate. Under this arrangement Japan and the United States, and other suppliers would have equal access to the Australian market but in return might be expected to take increased quantities of Australian butter, cheese, wheat, sugar, fruit, meat and other products affected by the enlargement of the Community. The third possibility is that Australia would abolish the two-tier system and fix a new rate either at the MFN level or between this and the old British preference rate, and negotiate whatever concessions were possible in third markets. In other words Australia would regard British preference as a bargaining counter to be used at the most favourable opportunity to improve her trading position and offset possible losses in the European Community. These changes could be made a means of strengthening the Pacific markets on which Australia is coming increasingly to depend, and changing the pattern of her trade away from exports to the United States and Britain.

SOUTH AFRICA

Although no longer a member of the Commonwealth, South Africa has continued to enjoy the advantage of Commonwealth Preference. It is estimated that about forty per cent of South African exports to the UK have a preference of around ten per cent, while one quarter of UK exports to the Republic enjoy preferential tariffs of four to five per cent. The main effect of British membership of the Community centres around the change in the system of trade preferences. Under the Treaty of Accession the UK will adopt the Common External Tariff in four stages, which will reduce the differences between it and the UK tariff to nil by 1 July 1977. South Africa is unlikely to be offered association with the European Community, so that exports which previously entered the UK either free of duty or at preferential rates will face the full Common External Tariff at the end of the transitional period. South African exports mainly affected are fresh and canned fruit, wine, sugar, preserved meat, maize and fish meal, which between them represent some thirty per cent of South Africa's exports to the UK.

South African dependence on Britain as an export market has declined considerably in the last decade. From the time of the 1961–2 negotiations for British entry into the European Community, South Africa has managed to increase exports to the Six, notably West Germany, and also to Japan. The proportion of the exports of the Republic going to the UK has dropped from 33.2 per cent in 1961 to 26.8 per cent in 1971.

In terms of South Africa's total exports, British entry into the

Common Market would not cause insurmountable problems. The main effect of loss of tariff preferences would be concentrated on a small number of local industries and the agricultural sector. In the wider context, South Africa's main competitors – Australia, the United States and Argentina – will be facing the same problems in the enlarged Community. Exports of foodstuffs, vegetable and animal oils, beverages and tobacco going to the United Kingdom represent only eight per cent of South Africa's total exports. It must be remembered that although increases in price due to changes in tariff are important they are not the only consideration in maintaining a share in an export market. Packaging, marketing, and quality are also factors which influence consumers and may outweigh price increases. Furthermore any adverse effects may be offset by steps taken to reduce tariffs in the GATT negotiations, and by arrangements made for the organization for agricultural products.

RHODESIA

The effect of British membership of the European Community on Rhodesia is largely hypothetical during the continuing embargo on trade. Like other members of the Commonwealth Preferential System, Rhodesia would lose preference at the end of the transitional period and her trade with the United Kingdom would be on the basis of the Common External Tariff and the CAP.

THE DEVELOPED COMMONWEALTH

The system of Commonwealth Preference, which British membership of the European Community will bring to an end, preserved a trading pattern which consisted for the most part of an exchange of British manufactured goods and capital equipment for primary products from countries better endowed with land and mineral resources. Apart from the commercial connection built up between them, the developed countries of the Commonwealth had a 'kith and kin' relationship with each other. Although the enlargement of the Community has been the occasion for a re-examination of the Commonwealth position, this had in fact been changing steadily over the past two decades. The effect of the Second World

War led to increased protection of British agriculture and a reduction in her dependence on imported foodstuffs. This in turn produced a chain-reaction from Canada, Australia and to a lesser extent New Zealand in the diversification of their economies and the search for other markets for their agricultural products. In spite of changes in Britain, the emergence of the developing countries of the Commonwealth as independent states, and adaptation in the developed Commonwealth, the system of Commonwealth preference continued.

One aspect of the changing situation which tends to be overlooked in the UK is the fact that the sluggish growth and poor record of the British economy has made her an unexciting trade partner for the developed countries of the Commonwealth. While trade with countries other than the UK has increased rapidly, the British market has become proportionately less important. Some of this change has arisen from the desire to diversify economies overdependent on the agricultural sector, but the fact that the British market was not expanding has been a contributory factor. All three developed countries have felt the impact on world trade of the growth of the Japanese market. With such a dynamic influence in the Pacific it was inevitable that the relative importance of the British market would decline. Without minimizing the effect on particularly vulnerable sections of their economies, both Canada and Australia have come round to the view that British membership of the European Community is something that they can live with. Only New Zealand is in the position where special measures are necessary if serious disruption of her economy is to be avoided.

The effects of the loss of Commonwealth Preference on the developed part of the Commonwealth may have a side-effect on the developing countries amongst its members. This would arise if Canada, Australia and New Zealand charged the MFN tariff rate on their imports from Commonwealth developing countries instead of the preferential rate. These kinds of change may very well arise but it is possible to make too much of them. Tariff policy is only one factor in determining the volume of trade between countries. Changes in exchange rate needed to keep payments in balance, and resources fully employed, can be much more effective in determining the volume of trade. Again a change in tariff policy in a particular market does not mean that an exporter to that market has the whole of his trade put at risk. To say that only 7½ per cent of Australia's exports to the United Kingdom are put at risk by UK membership of the Common Market does not imply that the whole amount of this trade will be lost to Australia. Again in the situation where Australian goods are displaced by European goods in the UK market, the pressure on the Australian economy is reduced as stresses in other markets where Australia and Europe compete is relieved. The same is true of Canadian trade with the UK. In discussing possible losses it is important to keep the relative size of the British market and of the Common Market of the Six in line. The Six are a bigger market than the United Kingdom for wool from Australia and New Zealand.

The key problem facing the developed Commonwealth countries in trading with the Common Market is the CAP. Although industrial tariffs around the Community are lower than those of the United States or the UK, protection against imports of temperate agricultural products is comparatively high and the system of protection is extremely inflexible. The variable levy used to control imports isolates the domestic market from trade fluctuations and denies the exporter the opportunity to compete by price reductions. The lower the price at which the exporter is offering the products, the higher the levy will be. Its effect is therefore much the same as a quota, and the Community will only import as much of a product as will sell at a predetermined price within its boundaries. Where Community prices have been set too high and surpluses result, then subsidies are paid to allow these to be exported at below Community prices. This result can be equally disturbing for the developed Commonwealth countries and the United States because of the disruption of markets through releasing high-cost subsidized exports. The notorious case of the export of 200,000 tons of Community butter to the USSR at a price well below that charged to the consumer in the Community is only the best-known example of the unfortunate results which the CAP can produce.

For the developed Commonwealth the fact that the CAP is now applied to British food imports means that they lose the advantage of their low costs in this traditional market. What has been done for New Zealand and for the sugar producers of the Commonwealth in the Treaty of Accession has simply been to postpone the date on which the full preference for Community producers becomes effective against their exports. Another problem is that higher prices may stimulate production in the United Kingdom. The White Paper estimated that British farm output might be increased by about eight per cent, with most of the expansion coming in cereals, beef and milk. If this happens then displacement of Australian beef, Canadian malting barley and New Zealand cheddar by home production by the end of the 1970s would appear inevitable, unless changes in the CAP take place.

REGIONAL BLOCS

Although the impact of the enlargement of the Community on the developing countries, particularly the non-associables, has attracted the most attention, it is possible that the problem posed for the developed Commonwealth will in the end produce the most far-reaching changes in world trading arrangements. One of the major problems posed by the enlarged Common Market and the reactions to it is the extent to which countries will retreat into preference areas in place of the multilateral trade under MFN arrangements which was the basis of the GATT. If regional blocs do develop then there could be groupings which would include Europe and Africa (the Yaounde and Commonwealth Associate countries); the United States with Canada and Latin America; Japan with South East Asia, Australia and New Zealand; leaving China and the USSR as the nucleus for political rather than regional blocs. This particular scenario leaves out India, which because of the enlargement of the Community is out on a non-associable limb. The blocs mentioned would each have a manufacturing base, sources of raw materials, and supplies available of both tropical and temperate foodstuffs. Experience in the EEC and EFTA has shown that trade within such blocs would develop faster than trade between them. It could be that monetary institutions might develop along with customs union arrangements, as is envisaged for the European Community. A development of this kind would involve considerable modifications, if not in fact the winding up of the GATT and IMF.

The regional blocs just described were on a North–South basis.

Another possibility would be to have a North Atlantic bloc containing the European Community, the United States and Canada, and a Pacific Group containing Japan, Australia, New Zealand and countries of South East Asia. The only problem here would be whether or not the various associates of the European Community could be included in a group along with the United States. Whether blocs of this kind materialize or not there is no doubt that the maintenance of the GATT multilateral system will be much more difficult as a result of the enlargement of the Community and the inclusion in its orbit of the various associates. Apart from the expansion of Community influence there are likely to be other bilateral trading agreements set up in other parts of the world. There is already for example a free trade area between New Zealand and Australia and Canada and the United States might extend the Automotive Pact to include other products. Both Australia and Canada have hinted at the possibility of granting preferences to Japan in place of those given to Britain under Commonwealth Preference.

In all this welter of possibilities it must be remembered that tariffs are only one part of the arrangements for varying and controlling trade. Eliminating non-tariff barriers, negotiating workable commodity agreements and above all setting up a stable monetary system are all of primary importance to the future of world trade. Not surprisingly, in view of the operation of the CAP and the damage which it has done to the trade of extremely influential and vocal competitors, the European Community is regarded as the main force working against world multilateral trading arrangements. In this situation Britain is in the hot seat as the country most likely to be able to influence the Community to adopt more liberal attitudes in its external commercial relationships. Whether Britain can exert any influence will depend very much on how far she is able to overcome her domestic economic difficulties, which in the first months after joining made it extremely difficult for her to accept the responsibilities and obligations of membership. If British membership of the Community simply serves to accentuate differences of view between members then it is unlikely that the Community will be strong enough to take a lead in seeking solutions to the problems facing the establishment of a stable trading system for the world.

5. The Community and the Third World

There is no denying the fact that the enlargement of the Community has greatly complicated the relationships between the developed countries and the Third World. The growth of a bloc of African states with privileged access to the Common Market, and the elevation to the same position of selected countries in the Caribbean and the Indian and Pacific Oceans, creates a discriminatory position. What is the situation of the non-associables and the countries outside the orbit of the Treaty of Accession? What adjustments, if any, are being made to help them to make their way in the new situation?

GSP SYSTEMS – THE PREFERENCE ISSUE

The idea that some developing countries should receive trade preferences for their exports to some developed countries has never been popular with those not on the receiving end. At the UNCTAD New Delhi conferences of 1968 it was agreed that a system of generalized preferences should be worked out to help those countries outside the existing schemes. On 1 July 1971 the European Community introduced its Generalized System of Preference (GSP), and in doing so was the first of the preference-giving countries to implement the UNCTAD proposals. The United Kingdom introduced a scheme to partly replace Commonwealth Preference on 1 January 1972, but in the Accession Treaty undertook to adopt the Community GSP on 1 January 1974. The differences between the UK and Community schemes are important as introducing yet another change in Britain's relationships with the developing countries, including the non-associables, as a result of joining the Common Market.

82

In the British system, tariff reductions equivalent to those enjoyed by Commonwealth countries were extended to imports of manufactures and semi-manufactures from all developing countries participating in the scheme (see Appendix 2). Cotton textiles and articles made from them were excluded, together with products on which excise duties are levied, notably hydrocarbon oils, perfumes, matches and cigarette lighters. A number of processed agricultural goods on a small 'positive list' were also included in the scheme. A safeguard clause enabled Britain to reserve the right to withdraw preferential treatment from any product of which imports rose to a level that damaged the market for domestic producers. This clause was invoked in November 1972 when import duties were re-imposed for a time on leather goods from Latin American countries.

The Community GSP

The GSP introduced by the Six, which had to be adopted by Britain and the other new members of the Enlarged Community by 1 January 1974, covers manufactures and semi-manufactures in BTN chapters 25–99. Preference on processed agricultural goods is limited to a small range of products. Raw materials and a number of semi-manufactures, including metals up to the ingot stage of production, are excluded. So are jute and coir products. Imports of manufactures included in the scheme are limited by tariff quotas (*plafonds*), and by ceilings (*butoirs*) on preferential imports from any one source or origin. If the level of imports rises above this ceiling, then tariffs can be reimposed. A distinction is made in practice between 'sensitive', 'quasi-sensitive', and 'non-sensitive' items, depending upon the degree of competition with domestic production in the Community. The decision on the action to be taken regarding these different categories of products is taken by the Commission. The different groups of sensitive products are treated by a different set of regulations. All manufactures except textiles and footwear imported from all developing countries are subject to restriction if the total imports exceed those for 1968.

The Community GSP has several important differences in coverage from that introduced by the UK. Whereas the British list of processed agricultural products given preferential entry was estimated to cover fourteen per cent of UK imports of this category from non-Commonwealth developing countries, their treatment under the Community is restricted to small tariff reductions on a narrow range of products. Associates of the Community continue to have duty-free preferences on products excluded from the GSP and on processed agricultural goods which enjoy partial duty concessions under GSP.

Although the intention, at least on the part of the developing countries, was that their exports would receive the same treatment in all industrialized countries, in practice both Britain and the Community retained elements of preference for Commonwealth members and associates respectively. A further point is that only a limited number of GATT members have introduced GSP schemes of their own. So far as benefits are concerned, those developing countries that become associates of the Community will be much better off than the host of non-associables for whom GSP treatment is the only trading concession. For these countries the Community GSP covers manufactures except footwear and textiles, with tariff quotas calculated as the sum of imports from all other non-Community sources in 1968. Ceilings on imports vary between ten and fifty per cent of these quotas. For those cotton and allied textiles falling within the scope of the GATT Long-Term Arrangement the GSP is restricted to seven developing countries, Colombia, India, Jamaica, South Korea, Mexico, Pakistan and Egypt. For textiles, tariff quotas are defined in terms of weight in order to prevent price-cutting. For 'sensitive' items in this category quotas were fixed at the weight of imports from the seven countries in 1968 with no provision for any increase. Ceilings are set at thirty per cent of the quota. For other textiles only independent developing countries can benefit, a decision which rules out Hong Kong.

Impact on Commonwealth Countries

The impact of the Community GSP on the Commonwealth countries of Asia, the non-associables, has been analysed in some depth in a study published by the Overseas Development Institute.* This comes to the conclusion that the Community is committed to preserving the measure of special preferences which existing Asso-

* Peter Tulloch, *The Seven Outside*, ODI, London, 1973.

84

ciates receive, and to extending its scope to African and Caribbean Commonwealth countries. It follows therefore that the larger the number of Commonwealth countries opting for association the greater the conflict of interest between them and the non-associables. This conflict will apply particularly to products in which the two groups, the ins and the outs, are in competition. These include such agricultural products as oilseeds and oil cakes from India and Malaysia, the seeds and nuts from Sri Lanka. Processed agricultural goods affected include vegetable oils and palm oil and canned pineapples from Malaysia and Singapore, tobacco and sugar from India.

How serious this situation will be for the non-associables will depend on how far they are able to sell their products elsewhere than in the enlarged Community. Clearly the Commonwealth Asian countries can export to the United States and Japan, but they will be doing so in competition with the countries of Latin American already established in the American market, and the African Community associates. However the loss of their preferential position in the UK market may prove serious for some products. Furthermore it may lead to a switch in foreign investment away from the non-associables to the African associates. For manufactured goods, India and Bangladesh stand to lose their duty-free access to the UK market for jute manufactures and face high tariffs instead. Indian and Pakistan cotton textiles on the other hand would have easier access to the UK under the Community GSP, subject to the operation of the tariff quota system. The ODI study summed up the effect on Commonwealth Asian exports of manufactures of the adoption of Community GSP as follows: Bangladesh and Hong Kong would suffer most, Malaysia and Singapore would be less seriously affected, Sri Lanka virtually unaffected and India and Pakistan could gain.

Benefits of Community GSP

The Special Committee on Preferences of UNCTAD has made an assessment* of the effects of the Community GSP after its first year

* *Review of the Schemes of Generalized Preferences of Developed Market Countries. Operation and Effects of Generalized Preferences granted by the* EEC TD/B/C. 5/3, UNCTAD, January 1973.

of operation, which gives some indications of its possible future effects. The degree to which developing countries will be able to benefit by the scheme will depend on the impact of two built-in constraints. The first, called the product problem, concerns the extent to which developing countries are actually capable of producing the products covered by BTN chapters 25–99. Those countries already exporting substantial quantities of these goods on an MFN basis stand to gain considerably. For those not already exporting, the margin of preference may not be enough to provide the necessary incentive to set up exporting industries. In any case the fact that a country was not exporting manufactures or semi-manufactures probably means that it had not the necessary political, managerial and technical skills to enable it to overcome the array of problems concerned with setting up manufacturing capacity, and also faced quality control, marketing, non-tariff barriers in the importing countries as well as the need to absorb the discriminatory element in the tariff. The first conclusion therefore is that GSP schemes, including that of the Community, are of most help to countries already able to manage without them.

The second constraint observed in the UNCTAD study refers to the significance of the preferential tariff margins, both with regard to size and predictability. For agricultural and fishery products preferential margins enjoyed by developing countries compared with the MFN rate are only about four per cent. This margin is regarded as too small to have the effect of enabling developing countries to expand their exports to the Community. For manufactures and semi-manufactures where the effective tariff rate is higher than appears from the normal tariff rate, a cut in the latter reduces the actual level of protection and helps to eliminate the tariff escalation between products at different stages of processing. The predictability of the preferential margin concerns the operation of ceilings on the total of imports allowed in at preferential rates. Imports in excess of the permitted amount have to pay MFN rates of duty rather than the preferential rate. As the ceiling is fixed in relation to existing export capacity there is no room for increased exports from countries already supplying the Community market, nor any incentive for creating new export capacity.

The rather depressing conclusion emerges that the well-organized multinational corporations operating in Hong Kong, Taiwan and similar developing countries will be able to profit by GSP concessions, but that countries seeking to industralize will get little encouragement from them. This situation will require careful review of the performance of the scheme in practice. If the Community market expands, ceilings and profit margins will have to be adjusted. The non-associates and non-associables will clearly not be satisfied with a system which discriminates against them all in favour of the associated developing countries, and against the poorest of them in favour of the more industrially developed of their number.

Trade under GSP

In practice, the impact of the GSP varies considerably between product groups as well as between countries. Some seventy per cent of Community imports from developing countries not associated in a preferential grouping entered the Six duty-free in 1970 under MFN treatment, so that only the remaining thirty per cent were in fact eligible for GSP treatment. It could be argued therefore that it was open to developing countries to raise the level of their exports to the Community simply by changing their commodity composition. Whether a particular country could in fact do this would depend on the structure of its economy. As nearly all dutiable agricultural food and fishery products are outside the GSP scheme, this adds a further twenty per cent of Community imports to the seventy per cent of imports already noted as not receiving preferential treatment. The UNCTAD study estimates that out of $2,444m. of dutiable EEC imports of products in BTN 1–24, less than $44m. are covered by the scheme. Of the remaining ten per cent of EEC imports from developing countries coming under the GSP scheme, about one third, consisting of industrial raw materials, are excluded from preference. Only seven per cent of total EEC imports from countries benefiting from GSP are products covered by the scheme. The commodity structure of EEC trade with the countries concerned leaves little room for increases above this modest level. If substantial benefits are to go to the non-associate developing countries there will have to be either an enlargement of product coverage in the agricultural and fishery section, BTN 1–24, or a great increase in their export capacity for manufactures and semi manufactures, BTN 25–99.

Information on the operation of the Community GSP scheme in 1971 published in the *Journal Officiel des Communautés Européennes* showed that the common tariff was imposed on only twenty-four products because the maximum amount had been imported under GSP arrangements. This number was considerably smaller than the conclusion reached in the integrated analysis carried out in the UNCTAD study. One possible explanation is that only a limited number of countries took advantage of the scheme in its early days.

The UNCTAD study, having examined the performance of GSP in its first year, concluded that the two countries most likely to benefit from it are Hong Kong and Yugoslavia, which between them accounted for forty-three per cent of EEC imports of dutiable products in 1970 coming from countries qualifying for GSP treat-

Table 1

1970 EEC import shares of major supplying beneficiaries under the scheme (per cent)

Exporter	of total Benef. Trade	LTA TEXTILES of covered products	of dutiable products	SENSITIVE of covered products	of dutiable products	OTHER M+SM: NON-SEN. of covered products	of dutiable products
Yugoslavia	28	not benef.		46	34	37	28
Hong Kong	12	not benef.		81	32	11	5
Brazil	6	not benef.		50	41	43	37
India	5	26	19	40	29	24	17
Rep. of Korea	4	35	34	75	74	9	8
Mexico	3	nil	nil	25	18	62	43
Pakistan	2	55	23	81	33	5	2
UAR	2	74	72	78	77	17	16
Argentina	2	not benef.		39	19	58	29
Singapore	1	not benef.		93	76	6	5
Total	65	—	—	45	36	24	19

Source: UNCTAD Secretariat calculations.

ment. Four other countries – India, Brazil, Mexico and the Republic of Korea – account for a further seventeen per cent, so that these six countries between them supply sixty per cent of this trade. So far as industrial products are concerned the study concludes that the only prospect of expanding their preferential exports is in the category of 'other manufactures and semi-manufactures' designated as non-sensitive. Prospects for other items are limited in various ways. Textiles covered by the Long-Term Arrangement (LTA) of the GATT are subject to 'voluntary' export limitations, and products designated as 'sensitive' are restricted by tariff quotas.

The import shares of the major supplying countries are shown in Table 1.

THE DEVELOPMENT PROCESS

Industrialization

The problems of development are closely bound up with industrialization. The exports of manufactured goods from developing countries represent only about five per cent of total imports of manufactures into the industrialized countries. At the same time they are approximately sixteen per cent of the total exports of the developing countries as a whole. While all developing countries are attempting to broaden the base of their economies by industrialization, success in exporting manufactured goods has been confined to a few of them. Ten countries – Hong Kong, India, Israel, Mexico, Iran, the Philippines, Pakistan, Taiwan, Argentina, and Brazil – between them provide nearly three quarters of manufactured goods to industrialized countries from the developing world. Of these ten, almost half the total exports are provided by Hong Kong and India.

One of the reasons for the lack of success of the developing countries as exporters is the narrow range of manufactured products which they have to offer. Nearly half the total consists of textiles, including clothing; other items of importance are leather goods, wood products, toys, shoes and sports equipment. Attempts to increase earnings from the export of manufactured goods have met with a number of difficulties which have proved

89

self-defeating. One is the lack of capital and skilled manpower in conjunction with the absence of managerial experience. Together these constraints have combined to reduce the possibilities of expansion. However they can be overcome by foreign financial and technical aid or by the organization of resources by foreign investors, which means increasingly by multinational corporations. Small size of domestic market is another barrier to the building of export industries. Those countries with large home markets, such as India, Brazil and Mexico, have a considerable advantage here, although in some cases the size of the market is offset by the lack of purchasing power.

These various problems are affected but by no means solved by changes in tariffs and other trade barriers and the introduction of foreign capital, all of which occur under agreements with the European Community. It is no longer possible to consider tariffs and their effects separately from those of foreign investment. In the past, foreign investment was frequently concerned with developing local raw materials for export. This activity, it has been argued, prevented the growth of the economy, and industrialization was neglected. After independence many developing countries introduced national plans and went to considerable lengths to stimulate the development of import-substituting industries. This activity depended upon importing foreign capital, technology and management, either in the form of aid or technical assistance, or from private corporations. In many cases the result was to set up industries that were capital-intensive and employed technology which depended on foreign expertise. This meant that the new industries operated on a small scale, generated little employment or income, and did not contribute greatly to the national stocks of foreign exchange. There has been a swing in recent years towards devising labour-intensive techniques for manufacturing industry, on the grounds that these would help build up effective demand in the home market and make possible economies of scale in sales to world markets.

A task for the EC

This is an area to which the European Community could give some attention. The idea of what is being called 'intermediate technology' has acquired widespread acceptance without making any considerable contribution to the practical solution of the problems of the developing countries. The search for the kind of technology and management appropriate to developing countries with their large surplus of labour has not progressed very far. This is not the sort of problem for which market solutions are possible. The World Bank has put forward an increase of fifteen per cent a year in the value of manufactured exports from the less developed countries as a target for the 1970s. So far it is not clear how, if at all, this task can be achieved. However if the international institutions, including the European Community and the governments of the developing countries, are convinced that industrialization through labour-intensive industries is the policy now to follow, then the international business community will no doubt adapt its operations accordingly. At present so far as production is concerned it is a case of anything goes provided it falls into one or other of the SITC categories.

Although some countries have lagged a long way behind, there is no doubt that exports of manufactured goods from the developing countries have expanded at a very rapid rate in recent years. As already pointed out, however, this increase has mostly come from a small number of countries. The conditions for success with export industries only occur in a relatively few countries. The situation is that large developing countries are able to obtain a fast rate of growth either in a relatively few export-oriented industries or in a wider variety of industries only partly dependent on exports. For the most part these conditions are not found in small developing countries, most of which are poor and whose markets are not big enough to sustain a wide range of industry or secure rapid growth in those industries which they have.

Tasks for Developing Countries

The number of things that a developing country can do in order to build up an industrial sector is limited. Four broad sets of activities stand out, however, as presenting opportunities for action. The first is the processing of local raw materials to add value to what would otherwise not be a very profitable export. The range of raw materials suitable for on-the-spot processing is limited, and in the case of, for example, some minerals, the processes used are capital-intensive. The fact that tariffs in the industrialized countries tend to be higher on semi-processed goods than on raw materials is a further deterrent to setting up processing operations.

The second major activity leading to industrialization is the conversion of import-substituting industries to exporting. The problem here is that domestic industries are generally highly protected and not in any sense competitive in world markets. Where a surplus is available for export this is usually the result of planning errors and the products available will not have been designed for export markets. The creation of customs unions and free trade areas covering groups of developing countries helps to create a home market big enough to sustain modern industrial plants. It is always dangerous to assume that manufactured goods can be regarded as suitable for any market no matter what their origin. The developing countries do not necessarily want carbon copies of the consumer goods made for the inhabitants of the European Community or America. Trade in manufactures tends to grow fastest between countries with similar levels of income per head. This means that exchange of products between developing countries is most likely to build up in products made with the particular needs of their populations in mind. On the whole, foreign firms operating in the developing countries are better able to move into the export field than indigenous firms. This is due not only to differences in productivity but also to their knowledge of export techniques and markets.

The third kind of activity which developing countries may choose to follow is the manufacture of labour-intensive goods for export. These products would be especially designed to be turned out in factories employing a high proportion of labour in relation to capital involved and utilizing various forms of intermediate technology. Some of the goods that might be produced in this way are toys, boots and shoes, textiles and sports equipment. However for the developing countries success in exporting generally provokes a protectionist reaction. This has certainly been the case in the European Community and America. If the Community GSP system is to mean anything it must be considered in relation to its impact on the economies of the developing countries. At the moment manufacturers in the industrialized countries are in a position to pressurize governments to keep out 'low-cost' imports. The belief dies hard that every industry in Europe or North America, however decrepit its cost structure, must be kept alive. That 'lame ducks' should be kept going in order to maintain employment, may in the short run be worthwhile. All too often however the long-term effects of diverting resources from expanding to declining industries must reduce the prospects for growth. The Community, through its industrial policy, should encourage the updating of industrial technology. The logic of this policy is not only that investment in the Community would be in capital-intensive industries with high growth prospects, but that the developing countries should have the chance to take over the task of supplying an increasing range of products manufactured under conditions to which the 'lame duck' syndrome does not apply.

The fourth possible direction in which developing countries can move towards industrialization is through the activities of vertically integrated multinational corporations. The advantages of this type of operation are that it provides capital, modern technology, and management and marketing know-how. As a result of initiating enterprises of this kind places like Hong Kong, Singapore, Taiwan and Mexico, which a few years ago were well down the scale among developing countries, have become major sources of sophisticated products, including valves, tuners, semi-conductors and other components and parts for the American and Japanese electronics industries. In addition, items ranging from clothing, luggage, gloves and wigs to automobile parts are all produced in these rapidly advancing countries. Other activities that bring the readily available and adaptable labour of some developing countries into cooperation with western technology are precision drilling of jewels sent by Swiss watchmakers (Mauritius), packing loose ammunition into cartons for the US Army (Mexico), and punching data on to tapes for US companies (various West Indian islands).

The range of activities that can be undertaken when know-how and management are applied to the labour force of the developing countries is enormous. Imports into the United States* from developing countries under items 806.30 and 807.00 of the US

---

* See G. K. Helleiner, 'Manufactured Exports from the Less Developed Countries', *Economic Journal* No. 329 Vol. 83, March 1973.

tariff rose from $61m. in 1966 to $539m. in 1970. These tariff schedules permit import duties to be levied only on value added abroad where the basic input originated in the United States.

The European Community has so far not advanced as far as the United States in the organization of multinational firms for exporting manufactured goods from developing countries. On the political front, multinationals have been attacked in UNCTAD and elsewhere on the grounds that they use their ability to switch production from one country to another as a means of keeping down wages. Another complaint is that they are able to exploit the resources of a country without any commensurate contribution, through taxes, to its development. The Yaounde Convention countries and the Commonwealth associables would appear to have a unique advantage in dealing with multinationals. This lies in the existence of the institutions set up as part of the Convention for the coordination of policies. The complaint against multinationals is that they are able to set governments of poor countries bargaining against each other for the advantage of having a factory established in their territory. It would be an advantage to both host governments and multinational corporations to have a forum in which policy was worked out. At present there is considerable competition in the offer of investment incentives by developing countries. A group of countries associated with the Community could with advantage cooperate in working out and applying a code of conduct applicable to both parties in the operation.

6. Developing Africa and Extended Community

Traditional Complications

Both French- and English-speaking developing African countries have reached a point where they have to make up their minds about their future relationships with each other and with the European Community. Looked at from Brussels, the main question seems to be how many of the Commonwealth African countries given the option to become associated with the Common Market will decide to do so. The eighteen Francophone countries are expected to negotiate and sign the Third Yaounde Convention and continue to develop their association with the Community. In fact the situation is not nearly as simple as this. For the countries involved, association with the Community is only one aspect of their external relations. The special relationship of the eighteen with France, and of the Commonwealth potential associates with Britain, have both been criticized as neocolonialism. Some of the African countries find it difficult to regard association as the first step towards a new or equal relationship between the Community and Africa. It is less difficult to see association as a continuation of the traditional commercial relationships between former colonies and metropolitan powers. In this context the enlargement of the Community is seen to have the advantage of helping to end the separation of African states into two blocs divided by language and with their communications channelled towards either France or Britain.

The year 1963 was a turning point for both French- and English-speaking countries. In January of that year the first British application for membership of the Community was vetoed by President de Gaulle, so that the Commonwealth countries, not all of which were then independent, had an opportunity to reappraise their position in relation to Britain as a possible member of the Common Market. For the Francophone countries 1963 was the year of the signature of the first Yaounde Convention. Five years later they signed the second Convention, due to end at the beginning of 1975, which brought with it the benefit of aid from the European Development Fund. This has certainly been of considerable help to a number of the poorer countries which are heavily dependent on outside help in developing their economies. Aid from the Community represents the greater part of the capital budget of states such as Upper Volta. By contrast the English-speaking countries are far more populous and economically stronger and are in the main developing faster than the Francophone countries. This could mean that if the eighteen become the thirty by the addition of Commonwealth associates the latter would, because of their greater economic power, be able to exert considerable influence in the institutions of the Third Yaounde Convention.

AFRICAN REGIONALISM

The East African Commonwealth countries, as members of the Arusha Convention and of the East African Common Market, in spite of the recent problems in Uganda, have already had experience at working together in a regional group. The possibility of setting up similar groups in West Africa is seen not as an alternative to association of the Community but as a means of securing faster economic development. Already seven French-speaking West African countries, associated with the EEC under the Yaounde Convention, have signed a treaty creating an Economic Community in West Africa. They are the Ivory Coast, Dahomey, Upper Volta, Mali, Mauritania, Niger and Senegal. Between them these countries have a population of about 28 m. and an area which is about eight times as large as France. The West African Economic Community will not proceed immediately to the creation of a full customs union because two of its members, Ivory Coast and Senegal, are economically much stronger than the rest. In the initial stages it will concentrate on organizing trade in agricultural produce. Preferences will be introduced eventually for a number of industrial products, to compensate for the loss of customs revenue, and a development fund will be set up. Beyond this the seven have not made any commitments regarding future developments. Their arrangement is by no means exclusive and does not imply any intention to end the links with the European Community.

Nigeria, the largest and richest of the West African countries, has shown a keen interest in developing closer economic ties with neighbouring states. The nucleus for this cooperation is to be found in the talks which took place between Togo and Nigeria in July 1972. The two countries have an outline agreement on economic union which other African states would be able to join. The Nigerians are not in favour of a Yaounde-type association with the Community, which they regard as an artificial barrier to closer integration between African countries. The fact that both the eighteen and the Commonwealth potential associates had to be prepared to start negotiations for the Third Yaounde Convention after the beginning of August 1973 meant that the time available for getting alternative arrangements off the ground was limited. Agreement to enter the negotiations does not of course imply a commitment to sign the Third Yaounde Convention, and it may be that a number of African countries will take part in the negotiations in order to explore the position fully. Some of them may very well decide when the time comes that the Yaounde type of agreement is not for them. Nigeria in particular has taken the view that in spite of the short-term advantages, including access to EDF finance, an association of this type is likely to further divide the Third World. However the object of the negotiations should be to improve the association between the African states and the Community, and it is to be hoped that too much stress will not be placed on the three options offered in the Brussels negotiations, and that the African states will take the opportunity to consider their position in relation to the Community in the widest possible context.

INTER-AFRICAN COOPERATION

The Yaounde Convention consists in effect of eighteen free trade areas between the European Community and the individual associated states. Within this arrangement two groups of former French colonies have attempted to maintain customs unions from

97

the pre-independence days. The first group contains the seven West African countries mentioned above and the second consists of four countries, Cameroon, Central African Republic, Congo (Brazzaville) and Gabon. In principle both these groups maintain a common external tariff and free internal trade but in practice they are able to levy internal fiscal duties on goods originating in other parts of the group. The Yaounde Convention does not exclude the possibility of a customs union within a customs union, or indeed of free trade areas between associated states and third countries in Africa. The stipulation is made that such an arrangement should be between countries 'at a comparable level of development' (Article 13). Third countries entering into such arrangements would not of course qualify for privileged access to the European Community unless they became associates under the Convention. So far the associated states have not made any use of the possibilities of forming customs unions or free trade areas with third countries under Article 13 or other articles of the Treaty which apply, for example Article 11 and 14.

The position of the three East African Countries – Tanzania, Uganda and Kenya – as signatories of the Arusha Convention has a bearing on a possible form of future association agreements. The object of the convention was to protect the export markets of the three countries in the European Community from the effects of the special privileges enjoyed by the eighteen AASM states, many of which produced similar primary commodities. In principle the Arusha Convention provided for duty-free entry of goods from the three East African states, and the Community members decided not to impose quantitative restrictions on imports from them, with certain exceptions. Agricultural products subject to the CAP were allowed in duty-free but subject to levies. Also certain products of particular concern to the Yaounde associates, namely unroasted coffee, tinned pineapples and cloves, were admitted under duty-free quotas of 56,000 metric tons for coffee, 120 metric tons for cloves and 860 metric tons for tinned pineapples. The East African countries for their part gave the Six tariff preferences on fifty-nine items at rates ranging from two to nine per cent. This reverse preference has been the subject of considerable criticism by the East African countries, and the estimated cost in terms of revenue forgone has been put at about EA £250,000. The Arusha Convention provided for preferences on exports to the Community worth EA £19.5m. in 1970. Some of these items were however liable to duty-free quotas or levies which nullified the nominal tariff preference. At the same time some of the major East African exports to the Community enjoyed duty-free entry in any case. These included sisal fibre, raw cotton, groundnuts and unwrought copper.

The Arusha Convention was mainly a trade agreement, but it also provided for setting up a common institution, the Association Council, and included machinery for arbitrating disputes where necessary. The arrangements made for the right of establishment and for payments were less comprehensive than those of the Yaounde Convention and there was no provision for financial and technical assistance.

AFRICAN DEVELOPMENTS

The attitudes of the AASM countries and the Commonwealth potential associates will inevitably be coloured by their past experience. The former will be defending a position of preference which they wish to maintain, while the latter will be securing entry into the European Community on better terms than those enjoyed before, while maintaining their position in the British market. However, discussions at the ninth meeting of the European Community – AASM Parliamentary Conference in March 1973 showed that the eighteen are by no means happy about their position in the Community market. Complaints were made about the operation of the CAP levies and the loss of preference because of the introduction of the Generalized Preference System under which non-members states benefited. There were also calls for increased resources for the European Development Fund, so that the eighteen would not lose because the Fund's scope was enlarged to cover the new associated states. In the wider context the eighteen are just as vulnerable to falling world prices for basic commodities and upsets in the world's monetary systems as developing countries not associated with the Community.

How far the present and potential associates of the Community feel that it is worth setting aside political scruples in order to secure commercial advantages depends on how these are claimed. At the European Community-AASM Parliamentary Conference it was proposed by Mr. Denieau* that there should be a Community scheme for stabilizing the prices of the principal basic commodities of the eighteen on a regional basis, with an insurance fund to guarantee a minimum income level to producers. The commodities concerned would be groundnuts, cocoa, copper, coffee and cotton. The scheme would be funded separately from the European Development Fund and would be an additional financial engagement on the part of the Community. A regional agreement on raw materials would greatly help the position of states dependent for their income on one or more of these products. It would not prejudice the conclusion of world agreements as it could form part of a larger scheme.

At the same conference it was interesting to note that the representatives of the eighteen AASM states declared that they wished to see the largest possible number of English-speaking states joining the Third Yaounde Convention.

THE COMMISSION VIEW

The view of the Commission regarding the future relationships between the Community and the AASM, as well as with the countries of Africa, the Caribbean, and the Indian and Pacific Ocean which could associate themselves with it, was set out in a memorandum published in April 1973. The memorandum is intended as a basis for discussion, setting out the characteristics for a model of association capable of satisfying the needs of all the countries involved. The Commission does not regard it as necessary for a single association to be concluded, so that it is possible that the Caribbean countries and those in the Pacific Ocean which decide to associate could do so in a regional group distinct from the Yaounde states.

The main points of the memorandum can be summarized briefly. The partners would have complete autonomy, and the conclusion of agreements with the European Community does not involve any limitation on their sovereignty or political development. The object of the association is to enable states working on an equal footing with the Nine to evolve a common framework for

* The commissioner responsible for relations with developing countries at that time.

economic cooperation. It is intended that the advantages already enjoyed by the AASM will be maintained, but this does not mean that no changes will be made or that there will be an absence of innovation. The free movement of goods in both directions will be maintained, but the Community is not demanding reverse preferences. The associate countries will be able to determine for themselves their tariff policies and, if they wish, to grant third countries the same advantages as the Community. This possibility in relation to tariff policies should be an important weapon in the hands of the African countries in future GATT negotiations. While continuing to recommend the conclusion of world agreements for commodities and raw materials, the Commission is proposing to set up ad hoc mechanisms within the framework of the association agreements. These would involve setting up machinery for compensatory transfers to guarantee the producing countries a stable and sufficient return for agreed commodities. These compensatory transfers would be used for the economic development of the countries benefiting from them, so that the Community would in a very real sense be operating a development policy and not simply providing aid and technical assistance. The products which would be covered in this way include sugar, groundnuts, groundnut oil, cotton, cocoa, coffee, bananas, copper.

The Commission memorandum also refers to the need to increase the resources of the European Development Fund while maintaining its principal characteristics. The problems here are to ensure that enlarging the scope of the Fund by introducing new associates does not mean a reduction of resources available to the existing eighteen. The main policy aim so far has been to concentrate aid on the poorest countries, and the French would certainly like to continue doing so. In this context some of the Commonwealth countries, for example Malawi, would merit consideration. At the same time the memorandum proposes that the EDF should contribute to regional cooperation in Africa by encouraging projects which affect more than one state. Another important change suggested by the Commission is that the resources of the EDF should no longer come only from the financial contributions of the member states but from the European Community's 'own resources'. These are the funds contributed directly to the Community by agreed contributions from the CAP and part of the VAT receipts. Such an arrangement, in so far as it was geared to income from the CAP, would mean that Britain bore a greater proportionate share of the cost of financing the EDF than under the old system of fixed contributions from governments. This is clearly an important area for negotiation involving the interests of Commonwealth Africa. If the EDF is to be financed in future partly from Community 'own resources' and partly from contributions of member governments, this could be an acceptable means of stepping up the total Community aid and development disbursements. However the principle of equity applies to donors as well as recipient countries.

The Commission memorandum refers also to the joint institutions maintained by the associates and the Six and proposes that these should be continued with appropriate changes to accommodate the increased membership. The new Association Convention, like the previous Yaounde Convention, would last for five years.

FUTURE PROSPECTS

The importance of the Community memorandum is that it opens up a number of possibilities for securing closer cooperation between the Nine and the associates in framing and implementing their development policies. For the Commonwealth countries in Africa which had been receiving something of the order of £70m. of British aid annually, it is important that any changes should be for the better. Certainly everything must be done to prevent a situation in which a tug-of-war develops between French- and British-oriented development policies. The African states do not want to find themselves in a 'captive' situation in relation to the Community, dependent on it for trade and development finance. It is for this reason that a number of French African states have defended the system of reverse preferences as indicating equality between buyers and sellers. However this particular problem seems to have been resolved by the change of Community policy away from exacting concessions of this kind from associate states. Under the new arrangements as sketched in the Community memorandum it would seem that regional groups could develop in Africa within the framework of the new Yaounde Convention and without prejudice to the associates exercising their sovereign powers in relation to the GATT and other multilateral institutions.

Elsewhere the Caribbean countries already involved in a number of economic groupings, notably the Caribbean Free Trade Area (CARIFTA), would be able to set up a Yaounde-type group with its own institutions. This could presumably include French and Dutch dependencies in the Caribbean, which are at present linked directly to the Community through former metropolitan powers. In the Pacific Ocean the small states of Tonga, Fiji and Western Samoa could also form themselves into a regional group associated with the Community with institutions on Yaounde lines. The fact that Western Samoa in particular of these territories has close links with New Zealand could raise interesting questions about the relationships of Community-linked regional groups and third countries.

In general the developing countries with the prospect of association with the European Community are more concerned about development than association. It will be for the enlarged Community to prove that association will bring to the developing countries not simply more financial resources but the prospects for development through economic cooperation between themselves. The division of the developing countries into associates and non-associables is therefore not nearly so clear-cut as might be supposed. The associates in English-speaking Africa have still to be convinced that there are advantages from looking to the Community instead of seeking advantages through global concession secured in UNCTAD. Experience appears to indicate that the Community instead of seeking to advance through global concessions does not rule out the fact that trading advantages may very well come from new developments such as the GSP from the GATT and Special Drawing Rights from the IMF. All this seems to prove that the negotiations for the Third Yaounde Convention will be, for the parties concerned, just as important as the Brussels negotiations were for the full members of the Community.

7. Community Aid Policies

In the preamble to the Communiqué issued at the end of the Summit Meeting held in Paris from 19 to 20 October 1972, between the members of the enlarged Community, the following general policy statement on aid occurred:

> The Community is well aware of the problems presented by continuing under-development in the world. It affirms its determination within the framework within a worldwide policy towards the developing countries, to increase its effort in aid and technical assistance to the least favoured people. It will take particular account of the concerns of those countries towards which, through geography, history and the commitments entered into by the Community, it has specific responsibilities. (Preamble paragraph IV.)

This statement is in line with the previous policy of the Community, which was to offer development and technical assistance only to those developing countries associated with it under the Yaounde Convention. A certain amount of aid goes to the French Overseas Departments and Territories and the Community grants some food aid to various developing countries in other parts of the world, in response to specific requests from them. The agreement made between the Community and the East African Associated States – the Arusha Agreement – does not include aid provisions. This means that the main characteristic of the Community aid policy is that it is directed to a regional group of less developed countries which in fact contain no fewer than eight of the twenty-five 'least developed countries' listed by UNCTAD.

The vehicle by which Community aid passes to the developing countries is the European Development Fund (EDF). Since 1964 loans from the European Investment Bank (EIB) have increased and reinforced Community aid. Under the first Yaounde Convention the eighteen associated states in Africa received a total of 730 million units of account, an average of 146m. U/A. Under the second Convention the total allocation rose to 918m. U/A, an average of 184m. U/A a year. A Unit of Account is one US dollar before the devaluation of 1971 under the Smithsonian Agreement. The associated states received substantial bilateral aid from individual member countries, notably France and Belgium and to a lesser but increasing degree from Germany, For the eighteen states, bilateral aid amounts to over sixty per cent and direct Community aid to about twenty per cent of the total official financial assistance which they receive.

For the poorer members of the AASM, which are not countries likely to attract private investment, it is a considerable advantage to participate in the EDF aid arrangements. It has been argued that because they are in receipt of official Community aid they are more favourably placed in relation to multilateral aid from the World Bank and under UNDP arrangements. In fact the Associated States receive $8 per head annually in official aid (Community and multilateral), compared with a world average of $4 per head of official aid going to developing countries generally. The resources of the EDF are provided by budgetary contributions from the member states. The EIB finances its loans from its own funds which are raised on the financial market. On joining the Community the United Kingdom subscribed $450 million U/A as its share of the capital of the EIB. The other new entrants, Denmark and Ireland, subscribed $60 million U/A and $15 million U/A respectively. This subscribed capital is paid up to the extent of twenty per cent, which is the same for the original Six, and the new member states also contribute towards the statutory reserve of the Bank.

BILATERAL AID

Another major characteristic of the Community aid policy is that it concentrates effort on a regional group of developing countries whose members are of especial interest to France. It has been the

105

policy of the individual member states of the Community to allocate their bilateral aid on a quite different basis according to national policies and inclinations. The EDF as the main vehicle for implementing Community Aid policies has three distinctive features. First it is a Community institution maintained by contributions from the member states which are dealt with in the same way as contributions to the World Bank and other multilateral organizations. Second the EDF is intended to supplement the aid policies of the individual member countries. Third it is democratically operated and the choice of projects and their implementation is agreed and carried out jointly with the governments of the associated countries themselves, in accordance with the priorities of their national plans. Aid from the EDF is on the basis of specific projects proposed by the associated states. Originally aid was limited to projects in the field of economic and social infrastructure, such as bridges, roads, ports, railways, schools, hospitals and similar public works. More recently, key projects in agriculture and industry have been selected for EDF financing. Rural modernization has been given high priority and accounts for some forty per cent of the total sums allocated, while the share for infrastructure has fallen from over a half to less than a third. EDF funds are also being used to help the AASM states to improve their marketing and sales promotion effort with a view to enabling them to sell their products more easily on foreign markets.

In general the EDF has operated in the same way as multilateral aid-giving institutions working on a global basis. It has financed over 5,000 km of asphalted roads, some 3,500 km of other roads, over 800 km of railways, and scores of bridges. Rural modernization programmes have helped create nearly half a million acres of plantations, together with village and regional developments, irrigation and improvement of previously underdeveloped lands and the sinking of some 4,000 wells. On the social development side some 10,000 hospital beds have been provided, together with schools for nurses and bush dispensaries. In the education sector, as well as providing primary and secondary schools and teacher's training institutions, some 14,000 scholarships have been awarded under EDF arrangements.

ASSOCIABLES AND EDF

In the arrangements made with Commonwealth countries so far – the Arusha and Lagos Conventions – there was no provision made for aid from the Community. If the twenty Commonwealth developing countries which have the option of joining the Third Yaounde Convention decide to do so they will take part in whatever Community aid arrangements it contains. The negotiations for the new Convention have to be completed between 1 August 1973 and the end of 1974, with the Convention coming into operation on 31 January 1975. Those Commonwealth countries deciding to take up this option will be involved in the negotiations. It follows therefore that as part of the new situation resulting from the enlargement of the Community, a number of Commonwealth countries will be receiving aid in the future from a new source not available to the non-associables. In this connection the views of the associated states will be extremely important. While it is tempting to suppose that the Treaty of Accession took care of all possible eventualities and provided a blueprint for future relationships, this cannot be taken for granted, nor is it by any means clear how far the Nine will want to concentrate their aid-giving activities on the Community programme at the expense of their previous bilateral policies. This problem has to be considered from the point of view of first the donors and secondly the recipients.

The Donor Countries

Before the extension of the Community the Six were routing an increasing but still very small share of their total aid through Community channels. In 1962, 3.5 per cent of the total was going in this way, and in 1969 8.6 per cent. The Community share of aid going to the AASM has increased, while bilateral efforts by the Six have remained fairly constant. Bilateral aid, apart from that of France and Belgium, was mainly directed to countries outside the AASM. Germany, Italy and the Netherlands allocated fifty-seven per cent of their net flows outside Africa. At the same time their contributions to multilateral institutions – the World Bank, UNDP etc. – were as large as or greater than their contributions to Community aid programmes. Of $855.6m. allocated to the AASM and French dependencies between 1968 and 1970, $670.8m. came from French contributions, and $108.5m. from the EDF and EIB. German bilateral aid went principally to Asia, particularly India, where it exceeded the British contribution. German aid and development assistance to African countries outside the AASM, was greater than to those inside.

Diagram 3. Total net flows related to GNP

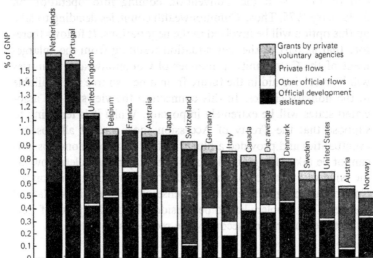

(Source: OECD Development Assistance, July 1972)

From the British point of view two questions arise. The first is how will membership of the Community affect the total cost of the UK aid programme, and the second, how will it affect the distribution of funds under this programme? The answer to the first question depends on how Britain's contribution to the EDF is worked out and whether the sum involved is given as an addition to the British total or would involve switching funds from bilateral aid. The criterion for working out the UK share in the Community aid programme will be a calculation of capacity to contribute based on the level of her national income compared with that of the Six but not taking account of the size of the UK bilateral aid programme for developing countries. The British GNP is about one quarter that of the Community, but it's rate of growth is much lower than that of the Community and productivity per head is at a lower level. The immediate situation is that because of the EDF method of providing aid on five-year commitments, Britain will not be called upon to make a contribution to the Fund until the Third Yaounde Convention has been negotiated. The EDF programme for the current five years will continue until the Second Yaounde Convention expires in January 1975. After that, Britain as a member of the Community will be involved in financing the EDF programme for the following five years. It is probable that Britain would be called upon to contribute some twenty-three per cent of the total sum involved. In an EDF programme of 2,200m. U/A this would have meant a contribution of some 52m. U/A*

A calculation of the British contribution after 1975 is complicated by the fact that no one knows how many of the Commonwealth associables will decide to take the Yaounde option and participate in Community aid arrangements. This raises once again the question how far the additional money required would come out of existing aid projections and would therefore be helping Africa at the expense of India and other South East Asian countries, as well as entailing possible reductions in British contributions to multilateral aid and technical assistance programmes.

The situation depends very much on the reaction of Commonwealth African countries. For example if Nigeria decided not to take up the Yaounde option this would mean a much bigger difference to the size and importance of the new association than if some of the poorer, less populated countries did so. In this case the enlarged association would be reduced to roughly 160 million inhabitants instead of 225 million. Under the Second Yaounde Convention the annual allocation of aid was roughly $2.5 per head, so that the absence of Nigeria would reduce the total amount needed annually by some $165m. If on the other hand a number of less populated Commonwealth associables decided not to take part in the Community financial and technical aid programme the result would not be nearly so significant. With the EDF at an intermediate stage and without any final indications of which Commonwealth states will join the Third Yaounde Conven-

* See *Europe's Chosen Few* by David Jones ODI 1973.

tion, the future scope and size of the Community aid and technical assistance programme remains obscure.

In the case of Britain it would seem likely that the EDF would be regarded as one of a number of channels through which British aid would flow to the developing countries. Its importance will depend on a number of factors outside the control of the British government, but it is clear that thorough re-examination of the British aid programme will be required well before the Third Yaounde Convention comes into operation at the end of January 1975. This review will involve a re-examination of the criteria for aid allocation, geographical spread of disbursements, and the relative importance attached to the various components of the aid programme. Not least, the importance of the EDF arrangements would be affected by whether the British government decided that effort should be concentrated on increasing official development assistance to above the target of 0.7 per cent of GNP set by the Pearson Committee and endorsed by UNCTAD. Official development assistance is a relatively new concept introduced by the DAC to cover official flows of assistance to developing countries, excluding export credits or private investment. It is measured by disbursements net of repayment of principal sums. In Diagram 3, which relates net flows from the principal donor countries to their GNP, it will be seen that official development flows reached 0.7 per cent of GNP only in the case of Portugal. For the rest the target of total outflows of one per cent of GNP was reached by the Netherlands, Portugal, the United Kingdom, Belgium, France and Australia, but in all cases except Portugal the result was due to the high level of private investment.

The Recipient Countries

The enlargement of the Community and the increase in the number of associated states will inevitably change the character of Community aid policies. Within the Six the driving force for associating the eighteen Francophone countries with the Community was undoubtedly France, whose relationship with the majority of the countries concerned was perpetuated through the association. Although the various special trading arrangements which the former French territories enjoyed in France, notably the 'Surprix' system, have been gradually phased out during the 1960s, the fact remains that the eighteen still maintain much close associations with France than with the rest of the Six. With the opening up of Community aid arrangements to Commonwealth Africa, Caribbean and other countries, the privileged position of the eighteen AASM states will be considerably eroded.

The probability is that the Commonwealth African countries, following the example of Nigeria in the Lagos Convention, and Kenya, Tanzania and Uganda in the Arusha Convention, would prefer an arrangement that did not include an exclusively Community aid arrangement. The ending of Commonwealth Preference and the introduction of GSP has underlined the independent status of the Commonwealth African countries. On the other hand the reform of the Franc Zone and the ending of the Sterling Area have at last made it possible for French- and English-speaking African states to enter into meaningful economic arrangements with each other. The indications are that the Commonwealth African countries would need to be reassured that the EDF represented a constructive effort on the part of the Community to rationalize its aid and development policies.

It remains to be seen whether introducing a further stage between national bilateral aid and global multilateral aid in the form of Community institutions will lead to more effective development policies. So far as Britain is concerned the real addition to existing aid disbursements is the amount which under a Third Yaounde Agreement would go to Francophone Africa. The eighteen at present receive virtually no aid from the United Kingdom, but a number of Commonwealth countries, including some in Africa, feature in the bilateral programmes of the Six. What will determine whether AASM and Commonwealth African states are better or worse off in the new situation will be the growth of GNP of the Nine and the way in which increased resources are applied in development programmes. The fact that the EDF is in effect a multilateral institution free to dispose of its funds according to its own internal decisions may very well make this form of aid more acceptable than that in bilateral programmes. There is no reason why the Nine should not increase their contributions to the EDF within a rising total of official development assistance. Again there is no statutory reason why the EDF should deal only with the

Associates. An EDF with a multinational programme which included the non-associables, for whom it could redress the harm done to their trading position by the enlargement of the Community, would be a considerable advance on the present situation. Clearly there is no lack of possibilities in relation to Community aid programmes, and these are by no means unfavourable to the developing countries.

8. The United States and the European Community

The relationship between the United States and the European Community is complicated by the position of America as the political leader of the non-Communist world. American involvement in defence, the maintenance of the world's currency and trading institutions, and aid to developing countries, together with its possession of the most technologically advanced industries, means that developments in Western Europe in the next twenty years are bound to have a significant impact on US policies. The continuation of American military influence in Western Europe after the end of the Second World War enabled the European countries to concentrate on their economic problems and disengage from world politics. In the British case, worldwide commitments based on the Empire were transferred into Commonwealth commitments.

The move towards a European Economic Community in the late 1950s was supported by the United States as the creation of a closely-knit economic and political union that would overcome the historical political rivalries of its members and restore Western Europe to economic strength and standing in world affairs. The objective as seen from the other side of the Atlantic was to establish an economic union large and varied enough to raise European living standards significantly, regenerate depressed and neglected areas, and help to develop the overseas countries associated with Community members. The Treaty of Rome was welcomed by the Americans as leading to a United States of Europe formed in their own image. In the early days the EEC was seen as a balancing factor in the East–West confrontation and a positive force in the world economy. The formation of the Community

113

was helped by the existence of American nuclear power and the availability of the dollar as the world's major reserve currency, and by the stabilizing influence of British policy in the transition to independence of the principal developing countries of the Commonwealth.

The combination of American, and to a lesser extent British policy, in maintaining arrangements for trade, aid and currency, enabled the Six, with France as an exception, to concentrate on building an economic Community. In doing this they behaved, 'as though they were living inside a charmed circle bounded entirely by their own problems and preoccupations'.* As time went on, and particularly when the enlargement of the Community became a possibility, the Americans began to shift their ground. Criticism of European policies, particularly the CAP, became more widespread. The Community's failure to emerge as a major political power in the world bore heavily on the United States as the problems of the Vietnam war and the growing deficit in the balance of payments made their impact increasingly felt. Two sets of problems emerged in American–European Community relationships. The first concern the effect of Community policies on the United States, and the second their effect on the Bretton Woods institutions.

EFFECTS OF COMMUNITY POLICIES

Setting up the European Economic Community involved drafting and implementing a whole series of policies aimed at securing economic integration. Although in the industrial field some matters such as pollution and safety standards are dealt with at national level, considerable progress has been made in drafting policies for the regulation of industry with a view to increasing the technological capability of the Community and removing barriers which prevent harmonization of national into Community practices. The position reached by the Six at the beginning of 1973 when the Community was enlarged can be summarized as follows. A virtually complete customs union and Common Agricultural Policy had come into operation. General commercial policies towards non-member countries were in process of unification.

* Andrew Shonfield, *Europe – Journey to an Unknown Destination*, Penguin, London 1973.

Harmonization of policies with regard to indirect taxation, depreciation allowances, investment incentives and the movement of capital between member countries were all in an advanced state. The Community had also taken measures to free the movement of labour between member countries and harmonize social security benefits. Work was in progress on a variety of common policies including those for energy, transport and help to backward regions. The Common Industrial Policy set out in the Collona Report of 1970* contained proposals to facilitate the formation of 'European' companies able to match the size, scale and efficiency of the largest multinational enterprises in the world. The Community has agreed, but failed to implement, plans for monetary union.

The measures taken to integrate economic policies within the Community have in various ways affected its relations with non-member countries. The enlargement of the Community, particularly the addition of the 54 million population of Britain and the need to fit its world trading arrangements into those of the Community, has added a new urgency to the situation. By the end of the 1970s, as was indicated at the Paris summit of October 1972, the transitional period for enlarging the Community will be complete, and common monetary and economic policies should have come into operation. It is this situation, with the Community enlarged and well on the way to integration to which discussions on modification of the Bretton Woods institutions must be addressed.

COMMUNITY IMPACT ON TRADE

For non-members, the fact that the average rate of tariff on manufactures and semi-manufactures entering the Community is relatively low is extremely important. As Diagram 1 shows, the United Kingdom, Japan and Canada, all have higher average tariff rates than the Community, which is itself only 0.1 per cent above the United States. However it is generally believed that the Community tariff is less protectionist than that of the United States, because tariffs on most products are around the average whereas in the United States there is considerable peaking, with some very high rates, particularly in chemicals.

In the period from 1958 to 1970, trade between the Community

* *Industrial Policy in the Community*, EEC Commission, Brussels 1970.

members of the Six went up from $8.2 billion to $43.3 billion, while exports to all non-member countries rose from $17.1 billion to $45.4 billion. In 1970 total Community exports exceeded those of the United States. Community imports from outside countries grew during the same period from $16.2 billion to $45.8 billion, a figure which was also greater than US purchases from abroad. To some extent, this increase in trade reflects the rapid growth of GNP within the Community. This was at the rate of sixty-seven per cent in real terms through the 1960s, compared with forty-eight per cent for the United States and thirty per cent for Britain. Exports from the United States to the Six rose between 1959 and 1970 by over 250 per cent, which was proportionately much greater than the increase of US exports to Britain and other EFTA countries. Community exports to Japan and to developing countries increased faster than those of the United States to these markets. Some trade diversion took place as a result of increased trade between Community members.

So far as industrial profits are concerned, it can be said that the United States was able to compete successfully for an increased share of the expanding Community market. This was particularly so in growth sectors such as aircraft, electrical machinery and pharmaceuticals. US exports to the Six increased as rapidly as exports to other destinations. In particular, American exports of non-agricultural goods as a whole rose by eighty-nine per cent, exports of manufactured goods by seventy-five per cent, machinery by two per cent, chemicals by fifty-three per cent and aircraft by 560 per cent. In view of this remarkably successful performance, it may be asked why the Americans complain about the expansion of the Community. There are two reasons. The first is that the level of the common external tariff of a customs union must be related to the duty-free conditions made inside it, and second to the situation before the customs union was set up. The introduction of duty-free trade creates a new element of discrimination against non-members, as they are competing with goods which move freely across what were previously national tariff boundaries within the customs union. The discrimination effect of a customs union is automatically raised when new members are added to it, particularly if they have large national markets, as in the case of the United Kingdom.

THE COMMON AGRICULTURAL POLICY

While non-members have increased their trade with the Community in industrial goods, the trend in agricultural products has not been nearly so favourable to them. This was to be expected, as there has never been a move towards general liberalization of agricultural trade comparable to that on industrial trade in the Kennedy Round. The Community's agricultural policies have always been highly protectionist and became more so as the policy was fully implemented.

Although American agricultural exports to the Community have grown to about one and a half times their level at the time of the signing of the Rome Treaty, the point from which changes should be measured is around 1966–7, when the CAP became fully operative for basic farm products. American exports of agricultural products covered by the variable levies and tariffs fell by forty-seven per cent from 1966 to 1969, although they rose slightly to 1971. The net decline from 1966 to 1970 was about twenty-nine per cent. Taking all agricultural products exported from the United States, there was a decline of only nineteen per cent from 1966 to 1969, and by 1970 the level had risen again to that of 1966. This was because of increased exports of soya beans, which are not covered by the variable levy system.

The CAP levies in the fourth quarter of 1969 averaged about 120 per cent on wheat and barley, seventy per cent on maize, sixty-three per cent on rice, fifty-four per cent on beef, and forty-five per cent on pork and poultry. Community prices for dairy products were several times those prevailing in relatively open markets such as that of the United Kingdom. Although it is true to say that the Six had all employed protectionist agricultural policies before entering the Common Market, the process of unification had tended to increase incentives to production, particularly in countries like France, where there was room for expansion. The increased incentives to produce offered by high prices, together with a rapid increase in agricultural productivity, have stimulated agricultural production in the Community to the point of self-sufficiency in most products. This has been achieved at considerable cost, and at different times large surpluses of grains, butter, sugar and other products have had to be sold on the world market with the help of export subsidies.

The system has operated to keep imports from playing any significant market role, except to bring in supplies of products of which there is a shortage. High domestic prices followed by high production not only displace imports but also produce surpluses for export. Efficient producers of temperate agricultural products elsewhere consequently have the problem of decreased access to the Common Market and also of finding new outlets for their products. This creates the absurd situation in which the traditional suppliers to the Common Market countries find themselves in competition with each other and with subsidized Community exports in third markets. In some cases the restitution payments representing the difference between the Common Market price and the export price have been higher than the world market price for the product. In early 1970 for example, the world price for soft wheat was about $50 per ton and the Community subsidy was $57 per ton. For products like butter the restitution price may be of the order of 400 ot 500 per cent of the market price.

The United States has also suffered by changes in the price differentials between wheat and such coarse grains as maize, which have made American feed-grains more expensive relative to Community wheat. This has meant that Community wheat surpluses have been used for feeding animals in place of imported maize. But the high price of Community wheat used for this purpose has led to increased demand for American soya bean products, so that it would seem the CAP has distorted rather than neutralized market forces.

The enlargement of the Community makes the situation with regard to agricultural trade more difficult for the United States, and for other former suppliers of the United Kingdom market, such as Canada, New Zealand and Australia. The principal cost of membership to Britain lies in the heavy contribution to the support of the Community agricultural system which will be adopted fully at the end of the transition period. The broadening of the coverage of the CAP will intensify the disadvantages already felt by American agriculture, unless the system is altered during or after the transition period. The general effect of applying the CAP system and its high price supports to British agriculture will almost certainly raise the level of protection in the British market, stimulate higher levels of domestic production, especially of grain, and lead to substitution of French and German grains for those previously purchased from the United States and elsewhere. This in turn will lead to an intensification of competition in third markets between the United States and countries previously enjoying Commonwealth preference, notably Canada, Australia and South Africa.

THE WILLIAMS REPORT

Various recommendations have been made for easing the burden of CAP on the United States. The Committee for Economic Development has recommended that the American government should protest about the discriminatory results of the CAP and seek modifications of the system or, failing that, compensation for the loss of markets. At the same time the United States should avoid taking unilateral action which results in distortions and increases barriers to agricultural imports. If progress could be made in this direction the United States should review the question of continuation of its special waiver in the GATT for protection of US farm products.*

The Williams Report,† published in July 1971, recognized the political problems standing in the way of quick solutions to the agricultural problem. European farmers, no less than their American counterparts, are anxious to protect their way of life and will not easily be convinced that a move away from the existing system might be in their own interests. The Report urged a gradual reduction in the level of agricultural protection, together with a generous programme of adjustment assistance for marginal and older farmers unable to stand up to increased competition without feather-bedding. Lower feed prices would make it possible to expand both production and consumption of livestock products for the raising of which European farms are relatively efficient. A lower level of dependence on subsidies would enable the costs of

* The United States and the European Community; Policies for a changing world. Committee for Economic Development (CED), New York, November 1971.
† US International Economic Policy in an Interdependent World, Commission an International Trade and Development Policy, Washington DC, July 1971.

the CAP to be reduced and ease the heavy financial burden on member countries, particularly the United Kingdom. In return for adjustments of this kind, the report recommended that a number of concessions should be made by the United States. One of these would be to release the Community from those agricultural tariff bindings, carried over from earlier tariff rounds, which had been nullified or impaired by the introduction of variable levies and other features of CAP and for which the United States has reserved its right to compensation under the GATT rules.

The Report recommended that the United States should seek to strengthen GATT rules and their application and enforcement in agricultural trade. A guiding principle should be that GATT members should not pass on to their trading partners the costs of their internal programmes of farm incomes support, which is of course exactly what the CAP does. The Report also recommended that the United States should act jointly with other members to secure the gradual elimination of export subsidies, quantitative restrictions and other non-tariff barriers to agricultural trade. In this context the variable levy is regarded as being similar to a quota because lower prices do not increase sales in the importing country. The variable levies also have the disadvantage for exporters that unlike quotas they capture the price difference for the importing country. In turn, the United States should demonstrate flexibility and restraint in its own actions regarding agricultural support. It could consider, for example, surrendering the broad waiver secured in the 1950s to permit imposition of import quotas. The liberalization or ending of existing quotas imposed under the Agricultural Act could also be considered.

The Williams Report also takes account of the problems of specialist producers in particular regions of the United States, notably the citrus fruit growers. It recommends that the United States should oppose regional preferential arrangements, and cites in particular the extension of preferential treatment to several Mediterranean countries by the European Community. On a general recommendation, the Report urges that agriculture should be given a high priority in the multilateral GATT negotiations. It regards the necessity to negotiate on the levels and techniques of domestic price support systems as justifying a sectoral approach on agriculture. As a general negotiating strategy, the report argues

120

that because agricultural trade flows are not balanced between major nations, concessions in agriculture may have to be compensated for by concessions in trade in industrial products, or possibly by measures outside the tariff field.

US FARM POLICY

From the reports of the discussions of the Council of Ministers and the European Parliament it could be imagined that Britain was unique in desiring to support agriculture by a system different from that of the Common Agricultural Policy. In fact the United States operates a system which differs both from the British and the CAP support arrangements. The American farm programme has three broad objectives – incomes support for farmers, the adjustment of supplies, and the stability of prices and supplies. Programmes for different commodities vary considerably. Wheat, cotton and feed-grains come under commodity programmes which together account for the major share of direct government payments to farmers. In 1970 they represented four fifths of a total of $3.7 billion. There is no direct price or income support for meat, poultry, fruit and vegetables, although these items account for about three fifths of the total cash receipts of American farmers. As elsewhere, a large proportion of the benefits of US farm programmes have gone to farmers with the highest incomes, who presumably have the least need for income support. In the 1960s, income per farm family more than doubled, but this was accounted for partly by increased productivity and partly by greater opportunities for farmers and their families to earn money outside farming.

The American system has been by no means free of faults. In the 1950s, surpluses of agricultural products were accumulated and substantial quantities were exported under the Public Law 480 programme. Even so considerable stocks remained. In this situation the price supports for wheat, feed-grains and cotton, the three main export crops, were considerably reduced in the 1960s. At the same time farmers received payment for taking some of their land out of production. As price support levels of these three crops rose to about world price levels, reliance on export subsidies has fallen and in 1969 was down to $63m. compared with $822m. in 1964. The Agricultural Act of 1970 continued the trend towards market

121

orientation and encouraged farmers to base their level of production on expectation of exports at world market prices. However, although the discrepancy between domestic and world prices has been greatly reduced and American wheat, grains and cotton are more competitive on world markets, abnormal situations still arise from time to time. In 1970, according to official estimates of the US Department of Agriculture, nearly the entire $900m. of payments to cotton producers was in fact an incomes subsidy which did not control supply. It is possible that smaller payments would have resulted in less cotton being produced. However payments in the same year to producers of wheat and feed-grains were regarded as necessary to prevent surpluses being produced at current price support levels.

If the criticisms of the CAP are to be pressed to a successful outcome, the American farm support system must also be reformed to remove anomalies. The Williams Report stated that present US farm programmes have been less effective than they might have been in helping low-income farmers and agricultural workers. It recommended the adoption of programmes related to the income needs of farmers, not to their actual or potential production. It also recommended, in line with the conclusions of the Food and Fiber Commission Report, that small farmers and workers who could not earn satisfactory incomes in agriculture should receive special help to enable them to move out of farming into other productive employment.

It is often forgotten that the problem of rural poverty continues to be acute in parts of the United States. During the 1960s some three million small farmers and workers left agriculture for other employment. If this outward movement is to continue then American agricultural policy will need to be framed to anticipate and assist adjustments. This situation, although in a very different context, is basically the same as in Europe. The Report of the National Advisory Commission on Foods and Fiber stated as long ago as July 1967 that, 'no reasonable or acceptable national farm policy could preserve farming opportunities' for 'those whose economic prospects are limited by the onset of farm technology'. Improvements in productivity through the application of farm technology have caused output per man to rise faster than the demand for farm products.

In the Community the need to generate incomes for small farmers has been met by pushing up prices, with consequent overproduction. In the United States the overproduction has come from improved technology, although errors in forecasting the amount of price support required have contributed to the existing unsatisfactory situation. The Williams Report is in fact going over the same ground as the Mansholt Plan and saying that the basic objective of farm policy should be to raise the level of marginal productivity and ensure that those who cannot achieve this find work outside farming. In other words the old idea of farming as a way of life to which men dedicated themselves must give way to capital-intensive, large-scale crop production with factory farming for meat and dairy produce.

AGRICULTURAL TRADE

On the trade front, the Williams Report emphasized that it was not feasible or desirable for the United States to liberalize its import restrictions on farm products if other countries continued to subsidize exports and to maintain import barriers that diverted large quantities of these products to the United States. The Commission recommended that as a general principle the need for protection against restricted imports should be met by imposing import duties and quotas. However for subsidized products, or those 'dumped' on the US market, countervailing measures to protect the interest of farmers should be taken by the US government. Although the government is urged to be tough with offenders abroad, the Report nevertheless recommends that the United States should negotiate a reduction of its import barriers if appropriate concessions by trading partners are forthcoming during the 1970s. This would mean that they as well as the United States would deal with the problem of raising farm income by measures that did not distort international trade. Transitional problems caused by these policies should be dealt with by adjustment assistance on the lines introduced by the Trade Expansion Act (TEA) of 1962. The measures proposed at the time were intended to alleviate injury resulting from increased competition from imports, and to facilitate the process of domestic adjustment by securing a more effective use of manpower and capital. Provision was made for workers to be

123

helped to change to new jobs through allowances covering a limited period of training or relocation, and through direct assistance in the cost of moving to new localities and setting up there. Measures on these lines would be applied to agriculture.

THREE PROBLEM PRODUCTS

Three product groups – manufactured dairy products, sugar and meat products – raise particular trading problems. American price supports for manufactured dairy products were raised four times between 1966 and March 1971. As a result prices received by United States farmers for milk are among the highest in the world but the net incomes of many small milk-producers are the lowest of any US farmers. In spite of higher price incentives there was a large and continuing fall during the 1960s in the number of American farms with dairy herds. In other words higher prices do not necessarily benefit the small farmers on whose behalf they are introduced. In this connection the Williams Report suggests a liberalization of dairy import quotas as a means of introducing price competition and reducing supply to an economic level.

International trade in sugar, as seen in Chapter 11, raises considerable problems both in regard to production and marketing. Under legislation going back to the Sugar Act of 1934, the US government has each year to determine the quantity of sugar needed to supply the national requirements at prices judged reasonable for consumers and fair to producers. Government also has the responsibility of dividing the US market for sugar between domestic and foreign producers by means of quotas. In the 1960s, between forty and forty-five per cent of US sugar supplies have come from foreign sources, mainly from developing countries which have received premiums above world market prices. This is in contrast to the European Community, where policy has encouraged domestic production of sugar and has cast doubts on the possibility of continued demand for the produce of developing countries. For sugar, as for other commodities, the problem is to secure the efficient use of world agricultural resources, and it would be difficult to say that any of the industrialized countries of the world have farm policies which have gone anywhere near to securing this objective. The Williams Report appears to take this point, and recommends that the United States should take advantage of the expiration of the Sugar Act, which occurred at the end of 1971, and modify its provisions so that a larger slice of the total came from imports and that the US consumers paid a lower price.

The largest source of income for US agriculture is the production of beef and veal, two products for which there are no domestic price support programmes. The legislation covering meat quotas contains a growth factor which allows imports to increase in proportion to the growth of domestic production. All the same, imports are a small part of total American consumption and might not increase greatly if controls were removed altogether. Continuation of the quota system, which has tended to restrict production of lower priced beef and therefore keep up meat prices for lower income-groups, has been a continuing irritant to foreign suppliers. The possibility of re-examining meat import restrictions is recommended by the Williams Report.

WHICH AGRICULTURAL POLICY?

The conclusion of the Williams Report is that US farm support policy has been less than perfect but on the whole has been better than the CAP. While this may be true, the fact remains that in both cases farm policies have been determined largely by political considerations, so that it is not surprising that they have been inward-looking. The Six have been able to introduce the CAP while the regulation of industry has been piecemeal and partial, because it is easier to enforce uniformity in the price structure for agricultural products. In fact the Community has developed an agricultural policy which satisfied the political needs of the farmers at the expense not only of foreign producers but of domestic consumers. The system based on high support prices has the effect of reducing non-member nations to the role of residual suppliers. The combination of high price incentives and technological progress, without any kind of production control, has meant continued increase in domestic production and the accumulation of surpluses which have to be exported at subsidized prices. The CAP has had the effect of raising food prices and therefore industrial costs, has displaced imports, increased self-sufficiency and had a disruptive effect on world markets for some products. Internationally the CAP is disliked because it forces farmers in other countries to bear costs which the Community policies should ensure were paid for internally. The result is that, 'European consumers eat less well and American and other farmers live less well.'* The American support system has also produced its surpluses of which some have gone to developing countries under PL 480, in the form of food aid, and some has been stored and released onto world markets at intervals. From time to time these stores have proved valuable in making good losses in production in different parts of the world, notably of cereals in the USSR in 1972–3.

The basic problems of the agricultural industry are broadly the same everywhere – namely the difficulty of controlling supplies at a level that will command prices sufficient to give farmers incomes comparable to those to be earned in industry. There is also the problem that support policies tend to benefit the wrong people and both social and economic objectives of farm policy tend to be upset when the further objective of avoiding undue dependence on foreign supplies of food is introduced. Trade in agricultural products has moved away from the multilateral trading system, and in doing so has created problems, not only for the United Kingdom, as the member of the Community most dependent on foreign food supplies, but for other temperate food producers, notably the United States, Australia and New Zealand, and for the developing countries.

POLICY PROSPECTS

Clearly there are no easy solutions to world agricultural trading problems. For temperate zone agricultural products a revision of the CAP is a necessary condition for restoring a measure of multilateral trade. Prices must be allowed to play a greater role in adjusting supplies and demand and preventing unwanted surpluses. For this purpose, tariffs would be preferable to using variable levies to protect high prices, as operated by the CAP. What is clear is that unless measures needed to speed up structural changes in the agricultural sector are not coordinated with support policies,

* Peter G. Peterson, *The United States in the Changing World Economy*, British North American Research Association, London 1972.

126

then the farm policy exercise is likely to be self-defeating.

It is important that international trade in agricultural products should not be disrupted while these necessary structural changes are being carried out. The International Chamber of Commerce has recommended a programme which would use medium-term action in depth to bring about the necessary structural changes in agricultural production and would enable a reasonable degree of price competition to be sustained. To this end a short-term transitional arrangement would be negotiated to normalize the condition of competition on the basis of the present situation, committing governments for a relatively short period of say three to five years. A new agreement would be negotiated before the end of this transitional period, which would take into account the progress achieved and the conditions of production in the various countries, both importers and exporters, and would aim at a meaningful expansion of world trade.

The essential feature of the ICC proposal is that if governments found that there was little hope of reaching agreement on basic changes in agricultural policy for the time being, then they should set themselves more limited objectives to deal with the worst features of the situation. The obvious general aim would be to introduce more flexibility into agricultural policies, so as to give foreign producers access to the markets of importing countries and an opportunity to share in the subsequent growth of demand in those markets. The acceptance of this limited objective would by implication mean agreement on extent and means of access to markets by exporters. The calculation of market shares inevitably involves an examination of support policies for domestic production and the effect that they are likely to have. For each commodity the allocation of the market between national production and imports would vary from country to country. An arrangement of this kind is implied at Community level in the agreement made for importing Commonwealth sugar after the transitional period ends in 1977. It may be that what has been proposed for sugar under the Treaty of Accession could be taken as a model for other commodities. This would require calculating a ratio between imports and domestic production based on the reference period and agreed for a definite quantity.

An agreement of this kind would have to include assurances to protect the value of the concession negotiated. When protection is by tariff only, it is possible to bind the import duties and prohibit the use of non-tariff measures and quotas. The problem is more difficult when protection is by variable levy or similar measures, and it can only be solved then if the government agrees not to intervene in the conditions under which the local product is produced and sold. At the same time it would be necessary for exporting countries to adapt their policies to ensure that output was related to the negotiated import requirements of the markets they supplied. These proposals clearly require a greater degree of international control over trade in agricultural products than governments have accepted so far. At the present time the international trade in agriculture products is a mixture of commodity agreements, regional and national trade arrangements. It may be that the eventual solution will take the form of a series of commodity agreements backed up by multilateral trading arrangements designed to produce a situation in which the conditions for equilibrium between supply and demand on the international market were met. For this to happen it would be necessary for all the major producers and importers of each commodity to agree on the way that it is to be dealt with, in international trade. It would be necessary to reach agreement on the use of the various means of regulating trade – notably export subsidies, sales on concessional terms (for example the Food Aid Programme), the financing of stocks and the use of safeguards to meet emergency situations.

The prospects for introducing greater flexibility into agricultural support policies and trading arrangements may be helped by a number of factors. The first of these is that the United States has already moved away from all-out support for inefficient marginal farmers and towards a capital-intensive, high-productivity, commercial-type agriculture backed up by adjustment assistance measures. Public concern at the high cost of farm programmes in the 1960s and the unsatisfactory distribution of government funds among farmers are other factors favouring a change in the system. In the Community there is growing concern at the ever-increasing price of foodstuffs, and the fiasco of the butter surpluses has demonstrated to the consumers the high cost of the CAP to them. The United Kingdom, used to a system based on deficiency payments giving the consumer the advantage of world prices, is clearly anxious to see an amendment in the CAP that would halt the steep rise in food costs that its adoption by Britain will inevitably involve. Farther afield in Japan a support programme for rice which resulted in prices three times the world level has been substantially reduced because of its high cost. This and other indications of discontent with existing agricultural support policies are not necessarily guarantees that changes will take place. However they do make clear the fact that the time has come for a serious consideration of alternative methods.

THE WIDER IMPLICATIONS

The enlargement of the Community has so far been considered in relation to the United States only in its economic implications. The international arrangements worked out at Bretton Woods were based on the realities of the situation at the end of the Second World War. In particular they enshrined the conviction that the United States was dominant both in size and competitiveness in the world economy and that the practices, institutions and rules introduced should be structured to fit this fact. Since then the American economy, although still basically strong, has lost its international competitive dominance and seen Japan and the European Community rise as major competitors. Responsibilities in the monetary and economic field adopted by the United States under the Bretton Woods Agreement resulted in a burden which could no longer be carried. The monetary and trading problems involved came to a head as a result of inadequate increases in productivity, excessive domestic inflation in the second half of the 1960s and the emergence of the growing deficit on the US balance of payments which led to President Nixon's new economic policy announcement of 15 August 1971. The meaning of this new initiative was a declaration to the rest of the world that the United States, though economically strong, could not by itself reshape the international economic system to cope with the changes that had taken place over the past twenty-five years.

What had happened was that patterns and practices were developing not envisaged in the late 1940s. The idea of multilateral trade based on the principle of non-discrimination and backed up by an international monetary system with currencies convertible into the dollar at fixed exchange rates was no longer a practical proposition. The difficulties encountered by individual countries, notably the United Kingdom, had repercussions on the monetary system. On the trade side, an accelerating trend towards regional arrangements developed, with the European Community as its major example. Adjustments to the system were made difficult because of the internal needs and preoccupations of individual countries. The Americans felt that as the principal supporters of the international system which had existed since the Second World War they were faced, in the European Community, with an organization that was trying to use international trade to further its regional ends.

It was not only with agricultural policies that the Six had discovered that in arriving at a generally accepted compromise it was the interests of the non-members that were easiest to sacrifice. From the American point of view the European Community has been largely responsible for the breakdown of the world trading and monetary arrangements operated by the IMF and the GATT. If something equally good is to be put into their place then it must be a system which takes account of the changes that have taken place in the last twenty-five years. So far the Community has been disappointingly inward-looking, and its efforts at integration centred around the development of a Community with political power have scarcely begun.

The idea that the old world, in the form of the Community, can be brought in to redress the balance which the new world represented by the United States can no longer maintain, is not yet a reality. The United States has increasingly demonstrated its impatience with the Community's inability to take up the larger share of the responsibility for operating the international trade and monetary arrangements. The crisis of the dollar, through its various stages from August 1971 to the Smithsonian Agreement in December of the same year and devaluation in February 1973, produced signs of an increasing willingness by the Germans to do something, but no clear Community initiatives to secure lasting solutions. Similarly the Japanese have shown that they prefer to make use of the system rather than help in its operation.

BRITAIN'S NEW STANCE

However, to say all this does not dispose of the case for bringing the European Community into being, or the way in which it is operated. If Western Europe consisted of states of the size and influence of Holland and Belgium there would be no problem about securing rapid and effective economic and political integration. The fact that it contained three medium-sized nations of around fifty million population each, France, Germany and Great Britain, all with the nostalgia of their days of grandure about them, meant that integration took longer and was less easy to secure. Britain has only gradually come to terms with the fact that the Commonwealth is no longer a cohesive economic system and that the member countries are fully prepared to look after their own interests. In this respect the Conference of Commonwealth Heads of Government in Singapore in 1971 represented a great break with tradition. The protracted argument about supply of arms to South Africa made it clear that Britain had the same freedom as any other Commonwealth country to follow its own foreign policy. In the past the British government has put the unity of the Commonwealth first and has on various occasions modified its attitude in view of the threat by one country or another to leave the Commonwealth. At Singapore and again at Ottowa in August 1973 it was made clear that Britain was now in exactly the same position as other members.

It has also taken time for Britain to realize that it is now free from the responsibility of trying to maintain one of the world's two reserve currencies. In the currency crisis of the spring of 1973, Britain was able to float happily on her own without accepting the need to adopt a fixed parity even for a joint float with the other Community countries. If the United States can be said to be adopting a sharper tone in its relationship with the European Community, the British in a minor key have shown themselves unwilling to accept all the implications of Community membership without argument. From trying to operate single-handed as a great power, Britain has discovered that much more can be done as a medium-sized power unencumbered with major international commitments. For this reason it is important that Britain should concentrate on

131

ensuring that the Community position is outward-looking in the widest sense of the term.

In doing this, Britain would find no shortage of problems. The Americans in effect have been saying since the dollar problem was brought out into the open in August 1971 that it was time the Europeans began to take up some of the responsibility for running the world's currency system. Not surprisingly, the Americans during the past twenty-five years have not pleased everyone by their performance in providing the world with its major world currency. Certainly the present problems of the dollar are due to the fact that so many people outside the United States were using it that the Americans lost control of it themselves. At the same time there have been considerable advantage to America, in the form of overseas investment, from operating the system. If is it true that the United States government has reached the point where it feels that it has to demonstrate that it can opt out of its responsibilities, we are facing a dangerous situation, as the Community has not yet reached a point where it would be able to take over. The danger is that some sort of piecemeal arrangement will be arrived at simply because the Community is not itself a unified political organization able to take on a world role. Such a twilight situation would not help anyone. The theory that anything that is bad for the Community is good for Britain, which some politicans appear to believe, hardly meets this kind of problem.

9. Comecon and Common Market

BILATERAL ARRANGEMENTS

Trade with the European Socialist countries – USSR, Poland, Czechoslovakia, Hungary, Romania and Bulgaria – is carried on under the framework of bilateral country-to-country trade agreements, usually valid for a number of years. This arrangement has applied in the past to trade with the Six and with Britain and other West European countries. The GDR follows the same general arrangement, but because it has not been recognized by all Western countries agreement has to be made in the form of non-official, trade agreements. Yugoslavia is a special case, as it is not a member of COMECON and has a trade agreement with the European Community (see page 47). There is also the difference that the volume of trade between Yugoslavia and the Six has been much greater than that of any of the other East European countries.

The agreements made between the COMECON members and West European states are essentially framework agreements which signify in general terms the intention of the government concerned to carry on trade within certain specified conditions. Lists of quotas are attached, which usually give the maximum quantity of goods to be exchanged in agreed categories. The expansion of East–West trade is hampered by two characteristics of the centrally planned economies. The first is that foreign trade is a subordinate consideration in planning economic policy and exports are only regarded as a means of obtaining the foreign exchange needed to purchase products abroad that are not available domestically either at all, or in the quantities required in the central plan of the economy, which is the justification for actually purchasing them. The second characteristic which occasions difficulty is the fact that exports and imports are balanced bilaterally, not multilaterally. Of COMECON

133

countries only Czechoslovakia, Poland and Romania are contracting parties to the GATT. Some West European countries maintain restrictions against exports from COMECON members by means of import quotas, and reductions in such barriers have to be negotiated on a reciprocal basis. In this situation, improvements in East–West trade cannot be brought about simply by changing MFN tariff rates. The direction in which improvement might be sought is through consideration of the ways and means of setting up joint ventures between enterprises in Western and Eastern Europe, subcontracting agreements, and other arrangements of this kind.

POSSIBLE CHANGES

The enlargement of the European Community is likely to affect trade with the East European countries in two principal ways. The first will result from obligations entered into as part of the negotiations, and the second from changes in the pattern of trade resulting from enlargement. Up to the beginning of 1973 the Six were able to make bilateral trade agreements with the East European countries. After that date all trade agreements with outside countries had to be negotiated by the Community as a whole. This applies to all countries, including members of COMECON. There is no East European opposite number to the European Commission, so that there is no COMECON central body empowered to act on behalf of the member states.

Relationships between the Six and Eastern Europe have changed considerably since the signing of the Rome Treaty. The principal changes took place after the Kennedy Round negotiations. All the East European countries now attend GATT meetings, four of them (mentioned above) as members and the remainder as observers. As a result the rules and practices of GATT have increasingly influenced the approach of the East European countries to trading agreements. International bodies such as OECD and GATT have played an invaluable part in improving East–West trade relations. In a different way the United Nations Economic Commission for Europe (ECE) has proved to be a useful bridge between East and West as it is the only European organization on which the USSR is represented. While it has been possible for individual governments to negotiate with each other relatively freely on a bilateral basis, it is only within the ECE that multilateral cooperation can be promoted.

TRADE POLICIES

The ability of the East European countries to buy from the Community is governed by the amount of their hard currency earnings. Trade policies are founded very largely on the twin rules of self-sufficiency and purchasing within the COMECON countries. In general, purchases from the West are made to satisfy two needs, first to acquire up-to-date technological processes and equipment, second to supplement resources of foodstuffs and raw and semi-processed materials. Demand for imported goods is increasing in Eastern Europe as a result of economic reforms, industrial development and the rise in living standards.

The trade patterns of the East European countries vary widely. The USSR sells predominantly raw materials and fuels, while Poland, Bulgaria and Hungary export farm products. Czechoslovakia and the GDR export a variety of manufactured goods. This broad pattern of exports places considerable limitations on the import capacity of the East European countries, as there is a wide gap between the list of things they would like to buy and their ability to earn the foreign currency to pay for them. One result of this stringency is that increased purchases of foodstuffs and raw materials are generally reflected in reduced buying of manufactured goods. This has been the case in the 1970s, when the USSR has been forced to purchase large quantities of grain from the United States and Canada because of poor harvests at home.

The currencies of the East European countries are not freely convertible, and this is sometimes given as a reason for the relatively low level of exports. The real problem is, however, that the exports that these countries have to offer either are not what the European Community, United States and other Western countries require, or are not effectively marketed. These difficulties are not likely to be solved by general discussion of the liberalization of trade. The problem is the fundamental one of bringing about a change in the pattern of trade between East and West, which will clearly take time. The fact that the USSR does not recognize the

European Community and its institutions has led to difficulty. While accepting the existence of the Community, it has generally mentioned it in disparaging terms and denounced it as a closed economic group whose aims were above all to strengthen capitalist monopolies and to act as the economic arm of NATO. This attitude has changed since the completion of the negotiations for enlarging the Community. The ratification of the treaties with the Soviet Union and Poland by the Federal German Government and President Nixon's visit to Moscow in May 1972 and subsequent American initiatives are all factors which have tended to improve the situation.

Relations between the Community and the COMECON countries will in future be on the basis of a common policy drawn up by the Commission and agreed by the nine member states. The first step in this direction is the stipulation that from 1 January 1973 all new trade agreements with East European countries must be negotiated by the Commission itself acting on the basis of directives issued by the Council of Ministers. In theory this would appear to require recognition of the Community by individual East European states, but it does not necessarily mean a formal recognition with the consequent appointment of Soviet and East European ambassadors to the Community. In any case the lack of recognition is unlikely to affect trade between the Community and COMECON significantly. In spite of the lack of direct relations the rate of growth of trade between the two areas in recent years was second only to the increase in internal Community trade. The share of East European countries in the total trade of the Community increased from four per cent in 1959 to 6.4 per cent in 1970. In 1971 the total trade of the Community members with Eastern Europe grew slightly faster than total Community external trade.

BRITISH/COMECON TRADE

As far as British trade is concerned, the principal trading partners among the Eastern European countries are the USSR and Poland. With the former Britain has a trade deficit with imports roughly double the value of exports. Only with Hungary does Britain have a consistent surplus. The main problem arising from British membership of the Community concerns imports into the UK.

136

Here Poland, with bacon and other foodstuffs forming half its exports to Britain, is particularly vulnerable. Hungary, Bulgaria and Romania are the other principal suppliers of foodstuffs. British acceptance of the CAP makes it difficult to reconcile the high level of imports of some agricultural products, particularly Polish bacon.

The position is by no means clear-cut however. The Six do not have a common list of quota restrictions imposed on imports from Eastern Europe, although this may be devised as part of the common policy for East European trade. One change that is likely to come about once the system of negotiation by the Commission on behalf of Community members has come fully into operation is the emergence of arrangements for long-term credits on a Community basis to finance trade with the East European countries. The object would be to enable them to import more of the sophisticated equipment which they currently lack, and also to make possible increased effective technical cooperation and the export of licences and patents. It is likely that more technical 'packages' will be put together to enable companies to sell know-how as well as equipment, on the lines of the Kama Lorry Project or the earlier Fiat engagement in the Soviet motorcar industry. Arrangements for the building of whole factories by West European companies would circumvent trade balance difficulties by making it possible for payment to be made by exporting some of the products.

FUTURE PROSPECTS

Future prospects for East–West trade must also be considered in the light of growing efforts to diversify exports from the COMECON countries. East Europeans see 'industrial cooperation' agreements as an important means of securing new technology, saving on hard currency imports, and developing new high-value exports – for example industrial components. The preponderance of agricultural products and raw or semi-processed materials in COMECON exports to the West is increasingly seen as offering indifferent long-term prospects for expansion. This also means that in Eastern Europe the need to improve hard currency trading, coupled with the decentralization and greater commercial freedom for enterprises arising from economic reforms in some of the member countries, is leading to a growing interest in up-to-date marketing methods and research.

It could be that the enlargement of the Community will lead to more closely coordinated institutional arrangements for dealing with East European trade, and possibly at a later stage with China. To some extent the problems arising from the enlargement of the European Community in relation to East–West trade are similar to those affecting the developing countries. Both areas require to diversify their economies so as to export more sophisticated goods and reduce the level of foodstuffs and raw materials in their total exports. These are long-standing difficulties arising from the structure of the economies of the East European countries and related to their monetary and industrial policies and the political ideology on which these are based.

The main immediate sources of difficulty are the CAP and the Common External Tariff through their effect on agricultural products and processed foodstuffs respectively. Where any large reduction in British imports from a particular East European country takes place it is to be expected that there will be pressures for reducing purchases from Britain. In any case a large proportion of British exports to Eastern Europe consist of industrial plant and machinery. This business arises from large individually negotiated contracts, often including a know how clause or other advanced technology content. In these cases pressures to divert purchases away from Britain because of a change in the balance of trade may be ignored because of the economic and technical importance of the contract.

In general terms a number of factors are likely to limit the expansion of trade between the Community and the Eastern bloc. The first of these is the increasing integration of the economies of the COMECON countries, which in the long term will reduce the demand for imports of industrial plant and manufactures. Secondly, the United States and Japan are increasingly active in Eastern Europe in competition with Community exporters. Thirdly, the high proportion of food and raw materials and semi-processed products in East European exports is so large that it will continue to be a barrier to the expansion of trade for many years ahead. This is because the most rapid growth sectors in international trade have tended to be in manufactured goods and machinery rather than in primary products. The impact of the CAP in increasing self-sufficiency in food production, together with arrangements for imports from associates and other countries, has inevitably decreased demand for these products from Eastern Europe. At the same time rising living standards in Eastern Europe should increased demand there for raw materials and more sophisticated foodstuffs.

For the foreseeable future, it does not appear likely that the enlargement of the Community will have any dramatic effect on trade with Eastern Europe. West Germany, which is already by far the most important trading partner of the East European countries, is likely to increase its lead over other Community members. German industry has developed very close contacts in Eastern Europe, particularly in the GDR, Czechoslovakia, Hungary, Romania and Yugoslavia. Existing trading and industrial relationships, and the close German connection and influence in technology, education and culture, should ensure that the Federal Republic will maintain its predominant position in the East European countries. The Ostpolitik policy of Chancellor Brandt is likely to support and intensify German trade penetration.

It would appear therefore that the Community and COMECON are likely to be absorbed each in their respective integration policies and problems and that neither will be in a position to seek active cooperation with the other. At the same time both Japan and the United States are likely to continue developing their East European trade. Both these countries require vast quantities of raw materials and fuels and are suppliers of advanced technology and industrial plant. If America and Japan run into difficulties in their economic relations with the Community they might decide to look more closely at other markets, including COMECON, but the most important factor is likely to be internal changes in the trading, pricing and financial mechanisms covering trade between the COMECON countries. So long as each of these conducts two thirds or more of its international trade with other socialist countries, possibilities for expansion outside with the Community or Japan and America are marginal. The need to generate increased earnings of foreign currency remains the basic problem of the East European countries. It could be that the most important development in East–West trade would be for the Community to coordinate the efforts of its members to provide the East Europeans with greatly improved credit facilities as a means of helping them to increase and diversify their exports to the West. A contribution of this kind by Community policy could go much further than the efforts of individual members in increasing their East–West trade.

10. The Community and the World Energy Problem

As one of the four major industrial powers, the European Community is a principal consumer of energy and resources. Without following the gloomier forecasts of energy resource consumption to their conclusions, it is clear that present rates of consumption of the world's resources are only possible for a small number of countries for a period variously defined as the end of the century or for a decade or so longer, according to the age and optimism of the forecaster. The demand for energy, which is a major indicator of development, brings together in a causal relationship the existing supplies and future use of the world's energy resources. The enlarged Community with its associates and trading partners in the developing countries is a major user of energy. As such it is in competition with the United States for fuel, notably Middle East oil, which has to be imported from outside its territories. At the same time the developing countries associated with the Community want to increase their consumption of energy as part of the development process. For these countries to increase their consumption of energy to anything like European, let alone American levels, would require greatly increased production of energy from all known sources and the development of new sources as well.

In industrialized countries the average amount of electricity used per person is closely related to productivity and the standard of living. The Group on Energy of the OECD stated that the electrical energy per industrial worker in the United States is twenty-five tons of coal eqiuvalent per year, compared with an average of eight tons in the industrialized countries of Western Europe. In developing countries the situation is very different, and it is only in capital cities or in exceptional industrial regions, such as the Copper Belt of Zambia, that the consumption of electricity rises to anything like that of the industrialized countries. The broad position is that the developing countries, with over half the total population of the world, consume less than ten per cent of its total energy production. This is a dilemma in which the European Community because of its overseas connections on the one hand, and its own rising requirements for energy on the other, has a key part to play.

The industrialized countries, defined as North America, Western Europe, Japan, Australasia and South Africa, produce over fifty per cent of the world's electricity and yet contain only twenty-nine per cent of its population. Whatever else can be said of the world energy position there is no doubt that forecasts for future developments are likely to prove at least as fallible as those that have been made in the last two decades. Technical advancement and commercial adjustments are taking place against a background of political change, so that a mixture of long- and short-term factors combine to produce a continually changing position both on the demand and the supply sides. On the demand side growth, industrial expansion and the rise of living standards are all pushing up the quantity of energy required. All of these factors, on any present-day calculations, will be working to increase energy demand not only in the European Community and North America but also in the developing countries. First experience has shown it is no easier to predict the likely course of development for traditional fuels such as coal and oil than for newcomers such as nuclear energy. Looking ahead the question is, how will this major international problem be affected by the enlargement of the European Community?

COMMON POLICY INITIATIVES

The Rome Treaty did not bind the Six to the introduction of a Common Energy Policy, and responsibility for energy matters was divided between the EEC (oil), the European Coal and Steel Community (coal), and Euratom (nuclear energy). Various initiatives, notably those of 1964 and 1968, were taken by the Commission towards the formulation of a Common Energy Policy. None of these got beyond an appreciation of the situation, and the circulation of information and statistics. The main characteristics of the

142

fuel situation of the Six were that sixty per cent of current requirements were imported and that individual members negotiated separately with OPEC (the Organizations of Petroleum Exporting Countries) for their national oil supplies. The Commission favoured a reduction in the energy imports by ten per cent of total requirement. This would have been achieved by checking coal imports, leading to an increased contribution by indigenous coal to electricity production, accelerating investment in nuclear plants and increasing exploitation of natural gas, both by intensifying the search for new deposits within the Community and increasing imports. The level of energy consumption by the Six at the time of the enlargement of the Community was 850 million tons of coal equivalent, compared with 330 million tons of coal equivalent in the United Kingdom. Over the last twenty years there has been a spectacular fall in coal consumption by the Six accompanied by the rise in the use of oil and natural gas which has kept the growth of nuclear energy production below what had been expected.

Dependence on imported fuel increased throughout the 1960s. Between 1957 and 1970 Western Europe as a whole lost an annual coal capacity of some 170 million metric tons. In Britain the coal industry is relatively more competitive than that of the Six, so that dependence on imports developed more slowly. However between 1960 and 1970 Britain's requirement for foreign energy supplies rose from twenty-five per cent of total energy demand to some forty-five per cent. In the United States, traditionally self-sufficient in energy, the requirement for imports rose steadily to a figure between ten and fifteen per cent of total energy needs. It was not until the early 1970s that the less desirable consequences of policies based on the assumption of unlimited cheap supplies of energy began to become apparent.

On the supply side, the dominant consideration had been the relative cost of coal and oil, with coal losing out to the readily available supplies of cheap oil from the Middle East and Africa. A rationalization of the coal industry in Britain and the Six was an essential stage in post-war economic development. The way in which it was carried out, however, ignored the special problems of the fuel industries. Decisions to switch over from coal- to oil-burning power stations have to be related both to availability and price of fuel over the lifetime of the equipment. As this is likely to be of the order of twenty-five to thirty years for coal- or oil-burning plants and twenty-five years for nuclear plants, planners find themselves under the necessity of living with their forecasts for a considerable time. Any appreciable increase in the price of fuel chosen for a particular power station during its lifetime could only be adjusted to at a considerable capital cost. The position is further complicated by new discoveries which change the pattern of supply. The discovery of North Sea natural gas and oil has been a particularly welcome change in this respect.

BRITISH ENERGY POLICY

British energy policy at the time of accession to the European Community was based on the 1967 White Paper *Fuel Policy* (Cmnd. 3438). This paper appeared before North Sea gas began to flow through the pipelines and when oil from the North Sea was not regarded as a possibility. The importance of the White Paper was that it moved away from an economy based on coal and oil to one in which natural gas and nuclear energy were added. Oil imports were still taxed at £2.20 per ton but the contraction of the coal industry was continued on the basis of the White Paper forecast that the demand for coal in 1970 would be unlikely to exceed 146 million tons, with perhaps a further three million tons for exports. Since November 1967, when the new policy was presented to Parliament, the fuel pattern has changed considerably.

The ingredients of a British energy policy are a mixture of indigenous and imported fossil fuels together with a relatively small production of nuclear energy, the balance of payments cost of the former and the opportunity costs of the latter. The proportions in which these ingredients have been put together, the methods by which they are produced and the degree of choice open to the consumer has varied according to political and economic pressures over the years. The common factor has been the continuing tendency for the demand for electricity to double every ten or eleven years, and that for petroleum for motor transport to rise by five per cent a year. On the supply side, the four-fuel policy of the 1967 White Paper has been overtaken by the discovery of North Sea oil and gas, the advance in the price of imported oil as a result of the activities of OPEC, and the dramatic changes in the inter-

144

national energy situation which have led to an increasing dependence on imported fuel by the world's principal consumers. A British energy policy for the 1970s must take account of the changes that have taken place in the price, supply and use of coal, oil, natural gas and nuclear energy. In 1970, coal accounted for forty-three per cent, oil for 48.3 per cent and nuclear power for 2.6 per cent of UK total energy consumption. Over the next four or five years the share of oil in total UK consumption will increase to around fifty-three per cent of the total, while the contribution of nuclear energy will rise by perhaps three times to 7.3 per cent or thereabouts of total consumption. Natural gas by the end of the decade will probably have worked its way up to between fifteen to twenty per cent of the total, which means that the relative share of coal, but not the amount produced, will have declined.

The British position is complicated by entry into the European Community. The Six have attempted unsuccessfully to formulate a common energy policy, and the arrival of Britain as a new member with abundant coal, natural gas and potentially North Sea oil supplies means that the balance of fuel production, consumption and trade for the enlarged Community is substantially different from that of the Six. In so far as the possession of supplies of indigenous fuel is a source of strength to a geographical area, the accession of Britain at this time takes on a new significance. One of the objects of establishing a customs union embracing major European trading countries was to provide a counterpart to the economic strength of the United States. In these terms it is clear that Europe needs to build up a substantial position with regard to energy supplies. In particular this involves European companies taking an increasing share in the oil industry.

Up to now the funds for exploration and exploitation of the world's oil resources have come largely from the United States. The time has now come when if Western Europe is to assume a position of importance in the energy field it must establish relationships with producer countries through trade, technical assistance and investment. European companies must press on with the search for alternative oil supplies in Europe and elsewhere. Furthermore they must finance and operate a greater proportion of the investment in refining, distribution and marketing of oil throughout the world. At the same time the maximum use will have to be made of indigenous coal supplies. In the United Kingdom this is being done through the large-scale research and development programme known as COALPLEX. This involves applying the principles of an oil refinery to coal as a raw material from which are 'distilled' a whole range of products.

AMERICAN APPREHENSIONS

Before looking at the ways in which a Community energy policy could be framed to accommodate the needs of the new entrants and associates, it is necessary to examine the international situation in which it would be operating. Across the Atlantic the United States, traditionally so richly endowed with coal, oil and natural gas, faces the prospect of shortages, immediately for natural gas and in the next twenty years for oil, if present rates of consumption continue. Part of the problem is the increasing awareness of the danger of pollution, so that energy policy is no longer concerned only with fuels as such but with those that are 'socially acceptable'. The same is true of the methods used to win fuels. In particular the environmentalists are now insisting that strip-mining techniques must be carried out in conjunction with land reclamation policies such as the National Coal Board has employed for the last decade. In the years when fuel was abundant, oil from the Middle East produced by American corporations and their overseas subsidiaries was exported to Europe from the producing areas. Now with increasing shortages these exports will be going to America, so adding to the difficulties of the European countries, which have come to rely on regular and cheap supplies of imported oil. The Middle Eastern countries between them contain some fifty-five per cent of the world's oil reserves. By the end of the 1970s this share may well have risen to around seventy-five per cent. The implications of this situation are clear both to the producing and the consuming countries. The former are becoming increasingly interested in downstream operations to enable them to sell the more profitable refined products instead of only crude oil.

The changes in the energy balance of the United States will have far-reaching implications for the Community. Inevitably the US will come into increasing competition with the Nine and Japan for the available crude oil supplies in free world markets. At the moment, although supplies are plentiful, the OPEC countries, which account for over ninety per cent of all exports, have 425,000 million barrels of reserves and an overall reserve-to-production ratio of about fifty to one. By 1985 it is estimated that the consuming countries will need some ninety million barrels per day from OPEC and other sources. To maintain a safe reserve-to-production ratio of say twenty to one, it will be necessary to develop about 480,000 million barrels of new reserves, after taking into account what has been consumed in the meantime. The size of this task becomes clear when it is realized that the Prudhoe Bay Fields in Alaska and the North Sea discoveries have estimated potential reserves of only about 20,000 million barrels each. If production is to keep pace with growing requirements then considerable new discoveries will be required.

Another aspect of this situation is the large and growing deficit in the United States balance of trade in fuels. It has been estimated that this deficit could increase from less than $3,000m. at the beginning of the 1970s to $25,000m. by the early 1980s. To pay for this massive increase in fuel imports the United States will need to seek additional export markets for goods and services throughout the world. To make good the deficit on fuel imports of $25,000m. would require an increase in exports by roughly forty per cent in value. The upset that this would occasion in world trade and its implications for other major exporters, notably the European Community and Japan, can be imagined. Apart from the changed pattern of trade there would of course be very significant financial implications for the United States balance of payments. At the same time, growing purchases by the United States and other countries of oil from the OPEC countries will create a major new sector of financial influence in the world monetary markets. By 1975 the eleven OPEC countries will be collecting oil revenues at the rate of about $25,000m. a year, presuming there are no major price changes in the meantime. By 1985, after allowing for growing price increases, their oil revenues could amount to as much $50,000m. a year. The fact that the OPEC countries have small local populations, relatively untried political institutions and great wealth adds to the difficulties of this situation. The pressures arising from conflict between the Arab states and Israel and the operation of the militant Palestinian organizations is another factor working against stability.

While it is possible to exaggerate the seriousness of this situation it must be remembered that its implications are not lost on the rulers of the OPEC countries themselves. It does not follow that all of them are bent on disrupting the world monetary system by using their advantages in an arbitrary fashion.

A COMMUNITY ENERGY POLICY

Community energy policy poses a number of questions for Britain. On the credit side, Community membership opens up the possibility of increased British exports of coal to the rest of the Community. Coal production of the Nine totals some 300 million tons about a quarter of Community energy requirements. Britain, with, an output of 140 million tons in a normal year, will be able to export increased tonnages to the Continent, working up to an estimated ten million tons. This prospect could improve the financial position of the National Coal Board by spreading costs over a larger tonnage and would also reduce its dependence on its principal customer, the electrical supply industry. Of the other fossil fuels, the discovery of natural gas in the North Sea is of considerable benefit to Britain and other Community countries, and should provide them with ample supplies for the next decade provided it is not used for purposes for which it is not basically suitable.

The relationship of a British energy policy to that of the European Community has to be taken into account. It raises the rather difficult question of pre-emption rights, which at present give the Gas Corporation the first refusal of any gas found in United Kingdom waters. Exploration companies cannot, without permission, export oil or gas discovered to any other country. It has been suggested by Community spokesmen, M. Fernand Spaak, Director General for Energy for the European Commission amongst them, that pre-emption rights should be at the disposal not of national governments but of the European Community as a whole. Much gas will flow before this argument is settled but it is another way in which Community membership introduces new responsibilities in the formulation of policy.

As far as Britain is concerned the fact that there is no Community energy policy is a considerable advantage. Britain, with the largest coal production and the as yet unquantified resources of gas and oil in the North Sea, should have a considerable say in future policy initiatives, and in determining the principles for a Community policy. The first of these is that a high priority should be given to security of supplies, which means ensuring the maximum use of indigenous fuels. This raises the question of what priority to give North Sea oil and gas compared with coal and imported oil. The commonsense answer would seem to be use North Sea oil primarily to replace imported oil rather than substituting it for coal in power stations. North Sea gas should not be used extravagantly but conserved by concentrating on premium uses. Nuclear power should be regarded as the long-term replacement fuel and every effort should be made to reduce the capital and running costs of nuclear power stations in order to enhance the competitive position of nuclear electricity. The policy of supporting coal which has been introduced by the British government should continue. In the background, but with increasing importance to the solution of the energy problem, is the question of research and development. This would clearly have to move onto a Community rather than a national basis. More importantly it should be concerned with energy requirement as a whole and not with individual fuels.

In the wider context of world as opposed to European resources, the major fuel-importing countries – United States, Japan, and the European Community – could cooperate in a number of ways. One of these would be to find more rational ways of using energy, but it is thought that this could at best only ease the situation until the mid-1980s. More important is cooperation in the search for new energy sources and their development. The European Community can help in coordinating the activities of the Nine, but as far as the other major users are concerned the OECD would be a better forum for concerting policies.

From what has been said it is clear that although a fuel crisis is likely it is not inevitable. The era of cheap energy in apparently inexhaustible quantities is over. For some time to come, higher fuel prices will act to keep up the level of supplies and increased research activities will bring improvements in the utilization of existing fuels and the discovery of new energy sources. At the same time constraints will be introduced from other motives, for example the opposition of the environmentalists to strip-mining at one end of the scale and to the proliferation of nuclear plants at the other. While the fossil fuels, the world's capital, are being run down, efforts to realize new energy forms such as solar energy and nuclear fusion must continue.

11. The Community in the World Economy

The preceding chapters have outlined the arrangements for enlarging the Community beyond the confines of the nine full member states. They have indicated a starting position and the regulations and procedures under which the extended Community will operate. The White Paper (Cmnd. 4715) concentrated on the European aspects of British membership of the EEC and understandably did not attempt to analyse the effects on countries outside. Its attitude is summed up in paragraph 61 which states, 'The enlargement of the Community would create a framework for more harmonious relationships in Western Europe. The relationships between Europe and the other countries of the world, particularly the United States, the Soviet Union and, one day, China, would become more evenly balanced. A Europe united would have the means of recovering the position in the world which Europe divided has lost.' This indication of the consequential changes that are bound to follow the enlargement of the Community is a statement of good intentions rather than policies. In Britain and to some extent in the Community countries, with the possible exception of France, the emphasis has been on what Community membership means to the national economy rather than what a nine-member Community means in a world context. In fact, the impact of what has been done in Brussels affects the world economy at both ends of the scale of affluence. The United States, Japan, Canada, Australia and New Zealand are all faced with a new situation just as dramatic in its impact as that involving the developing countries.

The insistence of the extended Community of nine full members on forming a sixteen-nation free trade area in Europe with the seven EFTA non-joiners, and making special arrangements with the European and Mediterranean associates, the eighteen existing Yaounde associates and the twenty Commonwealth associables, together with such trading arrangements as may be made for other countries, has created if not a rival to the IMF–GATT system, a bloc within it which has to be treated with special consideration. The complicated relationships of the Community and their impact on the world economy have two broad aspects. The first is the development of the extended Community of special associations and trading agreements with the non-member countries in Western Europe, the Mediterranean, Africa and elsewhere. This is the most obvious aspect of Community relationships but may prove to be the least important. The other is the impact of Community commercial policies and trading arrangements on non-member countries. This applies particularly to the treatment of temperate farm products under the Common Agricultural Policy and the changes that have taken place in the treatment of commodities produced by the developing countries.

The fact that the Nine constitute a market of 240 million people means that discrimination between commodities or manufactures and semi-manufactures from one source rather than another can represent a major dislocation of the international trading system. The developing countries outside the extended Community are now at a distinct commercial disadvantage compared with those on the inside. The introduction of the Community GSP System was the result of long-standing decisions in UNCTAD not directly connected with the enlargement of the Community. However the ending of Commonwealth Preference for manufactured goods, foodstuffs and raw materials was a part of the price paid for British membership.

PROBLEMS OF INDUSTRIALIZATION

In considering the case of the developing countries, it must be remembered that they themselves vary considerably one from another. A handful of them, including, India, Argentina, Brazil and Mexico, account for the major part in value of the output of manufactured goods from the whole group. Even so, developing countries produce only five per cent of world output of manufactures, a situation which is a major characteristic and cause of the state of un-development. Manufactures in this context are the items covered by the Standard International Trade Classification (SITC) Sections 5 to 8, less the non-ferrous metals in Division 68. The practice of talking about developing countries as a group has the effect of blurring the true nature of the argument. The schedule of preferences can have a very different meaning in one country compared with another.

As a generalization it is true to say that developing countries are short of capital and technological know-how and skills. However there is a great difference between the precise meaning of this statement in, for example, Brazil and Malawi. In general, developing countries are interested in production and employment and tend to be wary of international competition. Infant industries are protected and the domestic market organized in favour of their products. This principle applies also to the attraction of foreign capital or investment in new industries in developing countries. The brochures setting out the advantages of establishing industries in a particular country invariably specify some form of protection for an initial period.

Import substitution has generally been the starting point for industrialization of developing countries. Manufacturing for export markets is a much more difficult operation, posing a whole series of imperfectly understood problems. The domestic market on the other hand can readily be protected from outside competition and the new industries given a free hand to develop. Even so there is no guarantee of success, as inexperienced labour and management may be cheap but will also not be very productive. Also the home market, in terms of effective demand, will be much less than foreign manufacturers seeking to introduce competitive imports can count on. The economies of scale that should arise may be lost because the market is not organized to take the product, because of the way in which incomes are distributed or from lack of communications. The result is that governments tend to over-react and impose import duties, and quotas, or introduce the outright prohibition of imports in an effort to ensure that their infant industries will survive. In the developing countries with relatively large populations enough separate manufacturing units may be set up to create conditions of competition. Even so, difficulties arise when the industrial structure is broadened to allow for the manufacture of intermediate products. If this is to be done on a sufficiently large scale, there will be room for only a small number of firms in this field. In countries with smaller populations industrial subdivisions can be very difficult to organize and may very well result in technical inefficiency.

All this means that it is much easier to introduce some types of industry than others in the developing countries. The processing of indigenous raw materials for export can be organized more readily than the introduction of manufacturing industry that requires coordinating a number of different processes. It is not surprising therefore that industrialization has proved much more difficult than was anticipated twenty years ago. Looking at what has taken place, it is easy to say that infant industries have been overprotected, that tariffs have been kept high so that the beneficial effects of competition have not been felt, and all too often industry has been carried on in inefficient units too small to achieve economies of scale and making use of out-of-date or inappropriate technology. At the same time in most cases the national economy has not benefited as it should, as import substitution will most likely have produced a change in the pattern of imports rather than a reduction in their total value. Where industrialization has succeeded in raising the national income this has usually led to an increase in demand for imported goods which could not be produced by domestic industry. In fact of this situation, national plans, investment incentives and the whole array of aid and technical assistance have had less general effect than was hoped for.

How far does the extension of the European Community affect this general situation? The developing countries will be affected by the extension of the Community in different ways according to their position in the new structure. Three different sets of problems emerge. The first is the question of association and the way in which this affects the relationship of developing countries generally with the Community; the second is the effect of the Common Agricultural Policy on the trade of the developing countries; and the third, the effect of the GSP Scheme as applied by the Nine.

154

ASSOCIATION AND NON-ASSOCIATION

Perhaps the most important point about the association of Commonwealth developing countries with the Community is that while appearing to perpetuate the existing relationship the negotiations had the effect of excluding the greater part of Commonwealth population from a vast new preferential commercial arrangement. The second point is that the associable stakes have a commercial interest over the greater part of Africa as far south as the Zambezi. In other words the selection of both the outs and the ins will have far-reaching effects on the future pattern of world trading relationships.

Association is based on the principle of establishing a free trade area with reciprocal rights and obligations between the Community and each associated country. This means that where Community preferences are granted on imports from associates the latter are also required to grant reverse preferences on imports from the Community. Reverse preferences have been criticized by the United States as being contrary to the GATT and by the developing countries concerned as preventing them from buying in the cheapest markets. A further criticism is that the system perpetuates the old colonial arrangement under which the developing countries were exporters of primary products and importers of manufactured goods. The abolition of reverse preferences would not affect a very large volume of trade so far as the Yaounde states are concerned, nor indeed for many of the Commonwealth African associable countries. Against this some of these Yaounde countries are prepared to argue that reverse preferences provide the moral basis for association, in that they recognize the sovereign status of the developing country associates. In addition the French, who were largely responsible for putting up the system in the first place, are reluctant to lose their entrenched trading positions in the Francophone countries.

The GATT position is that its rules provide that the only two ways in which the Community can give preferential access to the exports of the associates are either to obtain a waiver in GATT or to establish a free trade area. The prospects of obtaining a waiver are very slight, in view of opposition from the United States and from those developing countries excluded from association agreements.

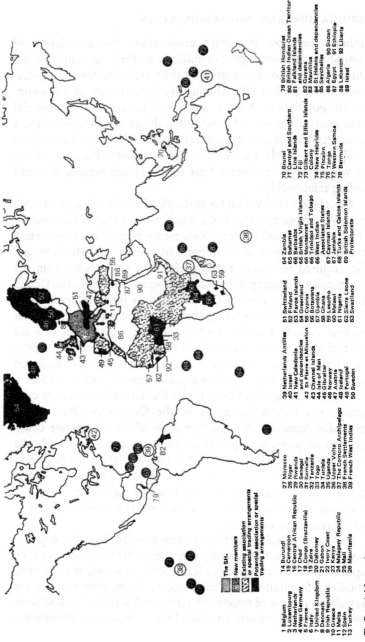

The Extended Community

Members Present and Potential, Associates,Dependencies.

The SIX.

New members

Existing association
or special trading arrangements

Potential association or special
trading arrangements

1 Belgium
2 Luxembourg
3 Netherlands
4 West Germany
5 France
6 Italy
7 United Kingdom
8 Denmark
9 Irish Republic
10 Greece
11 Malta
12 Spain
13 Turkey

14 Burundi
15 Cameroon
16 Central African Republic
17 Chad
18 Congo (Brazzaville)
19 Zaire
20 Dahomey
21 Gabon
22 Ivory Coast
23 Kenya
24 Malagasy Republic
25 Mali
26 Mauritania

27 Morocco
28 Niger
29 Rwanda
30 Senegal
31 Somalia
32 Tanzania
33 Togo
34 Tunisia
35 Uganda
36 Upper Volta
37 The Comoro Archipelago
38 French Settlements
39 French West Indies

39 Netherlands Antilles
40 Israel
41 New Caledonia
and dependencies
42 St Pierre et Miquelon
43 Channel Islands
44 Isle of Man
45 Gibraltar
46 Norway
47 Austria
48 Iceland
49 Portugal
50 Sweden

51 Switzerland
52 Finland
53 Faroe Islands
54 Greenland
55 Cyprus
56 Botswana
57 Gambia
58 Ghana
59 Lesotho
60 Malawi
61 Nigeria
62 Sierra Leone
63 Swaziland

64 Zambia
65 Bahamas
66 Barbados
66 British Virgin Islands
66 Montserrat
66 Trinidad and Tobago
66 West Indian
Associated States
67 Cayman Islands
67 Jamaica
68 Turks and Caicos Islands
69 British Solomon Islands
Protectorate

70 Brunei
71 Central and Southern
Line Islands
72 Fiji
73 Gilbert and Ellice Islands
Colony
74 New Hebrides
75 Pitcairn
76 Tonga
77 Western Samoa
78 Bermuda

79 British Honduras
80 British Indian Ocean Territory
and dependencies
81 Falkland Islands
82 Guyana
83 Mauritius
84 St Helena and dependencies
85 Seychelles
86 Algeria
87 Egypt
88 Lebanon
89 Israel
90 Sudan
91 Ethiopia
92 Liberia

This explains why the somewhat cumbersome arrangement of a series of free trade areas was adopted in the first place and was extended to cover the new situation. A compromise proposal has been prepared by the Community Secretariat in a paper drawn up by Herr H. B. Krohn, under which associates would reduce their tariffs to zero on European exports in exchange for low tariffs on imports of their products into the Community. At the same time associates would be free to offer the same tariff to the rest of the world as to the Community. The difficulty of this is that a low tariff means a serious loss of revenue to the associates and in their view would discourage their infant industries. To get over this problem it has been suggested that they should be free to impose fiscal duties which they can set at any figure they like, in addition to a low rate of tariff duty. This fiscal duty would apply to imports from the Community and from the rest of the world. The ability to impose a duty of this kind would give the associate countries power to operate a free trade zone by having low tariff duties, but in practice to regulate imports by means of fiscal duties. From the point of view of the non-associables this arrangement would look rather less attractive, as it provides the associates with considerable access to the Community markets, an advantage denied to non-associables, and at the same time flexibility in protecting their home markets.

Although the offer of association to Commonwealth African and other countries appears to have great advantages it remains to be seen what these will be in practice. The policy of preferential access to the Community covers only a small proportion of world trade and was for that reason regarded as feasible in Community doctrine. Obviously if too many countries become associated the benefits will be diluted for the participants while the scale of distortion and difficulties in world trade generally will increase. This was the thinking behind the exclusion of the Commonwealth Asian countries, which was probably affected by the fact that in Africa, Nigeria alone contained a much larger population than all the Yaounde countries put together. The non-associables have to be content with the extension of generalized preferences as some compensation for their exclusion from the extended Community. These benefits depend largely on whether all other industrialized countries extend preferences on a similar scale to those of the

Community. The delay in implementing the United States' GSP scheme and the exclusion of a number of important manufactures such as textiles and leather goods from existing schemes is a considerable disadvantage to the Commonwealth Asian countries. Much will depend on the outcome of the negotiations for special trading arrangements for particular products, notably jute, coir, handicrafts and textiles, which India and Pakistan have opened with the Community. While the benefits of association and the disadvantages of non-association will only emerge fully with the passage of time, there is no doubt that for Community purposes the developing countries are now divided into two classes, a fact which must have repercussions on the organization of the world economy generally.

EXPORTS OF MANUFACTURERS

Although manufactured goods account for less than a quarter of total exports by value of the developing countries, they are important because they offer the best prospects for improving export performance. The demand for manufactures, unlike that for agricultural products, is growing rapidly, and developing countries' exports of them increased at an annual rate of fifteen per cent during the 1960s. The particular types of manufacture which developing countries are best able to cope with are textiles, footwear and artisan products, all of which are labour-intensive. In addition a number of newer products are now being turned out, including plywood, paper products and fabricated metals. In some cases developing countries are successfully engaged in certain production processes such as manufacturing components, assembly and packaging. Only a very few of them, such as Hong Kong and Singapore, have managed to break through into exporting more sophisticated manufactured goods.

In selling their manufactured goods overseas, the developing countries come up against the problem posed by the fact that labour-intensive industries are given a high level of protection in industrialized countries, either by quotas, tariffs or 'orderly marketing arrangements'. The situation continues in spite of the fact that these imports represent only a small proportion of imports of manufactures from all sources by industralized countries.

Protection is made all the more difficult for developing countries by the structure of tariff systems under which the rate of duty increases with the degree of processing. Even if the tariff on the raw material is zero it is possible to end up with a high duty on semi-processed or finished articles made from it.

AGRICULTURAL POLICY

While the share in world trade of the exports of manufactures from developing countries is increasing slowly, those of primary and processed agricultural products are falling. This is particularly so where developing and industrialized countries alike are producers, as in the case of wheat, oils and fats, and sugar. The industrialized countries have all protected their farmers from foreign competition in one way or another, but the British system at least had the merit of enabling purchases to be made in the world market. For the developing countries, exports of primary products account for three times as much as manufactured goods as earners of foreign exchange. Even when oil is excluded from the calculation they still earn twice as much. The importance of primary products is heightened by the fact that seven developing countries supply two thirds of the total of manufactures from all such countries. Exports of food and raw materials face a variety of difficulties apart from the various protective measures encountered. Some of them are subject to sudden fluctuations in demand and export earnings. Because of their nature, a rise in world incomes does not generally lead to a corresponding increase in demand for primary products. Indeed because of the delay before increased spending works its way through to food and raw materials, the proportion of total income spent on them actually falls. However if demand for a particular raw material rises so that producers find themselves enjoying higher incomes for a change, the search for synthetic substitutes for their product is stepped up, and prices are forced down. This has happened at various times to wool, cotton, jute and rubber. With countries as with people, the rich tend to get richer and the poor poorer.

The Common Agricultural Policy has come under criticism in the Community because of its high cost both to the consumer at the point of sale, and governments in the cost of price support. Non-member countries regard the CAP as a major distortion of world trade and indirectly of the international monetary system. The operation of CAP under the old six-nation Community was bearable because the member countries had reached a high level of self-sufficiency. The entry of the United Kingdom poses more far-reaching problems. The key to the new situation is the fact that Britain is a net importer of food while the Six as a group were a net exporter. The acceptance of the CAP by Britain as a condition of entry inevitably means that future import requirements will be met increasingly from the Six. This diversion of production and trade will take place at the expense of consumers in the Six generally, taxpayers particularly in Britain, and foreign food-producers. No one has been able to produce a convincing argument in favour of the application of the CAP to British agriculture, except of course producers in the Six. The fact that Britain presents a mirror image of the Six in its trade and production of foodstuffs means that the adoption of CAP will be a costly operation for which compensation must be sought in other sectors.

Traditionally, British farm policy was constructed to produce a balance between the interests of the consumer who benefited from low prices under the agricultural support policies, the domestic producers who received a price agreed at the annual farm review, and the foreign producer who had free access to the British market. In addition to the low or zero tariffs on foodstuffs on which this arrangement relied, there were preferences on many items for Commonwealth suppliers. Ireland benefited under the Anglo-Irish Trade Treaty and Denmark under special arrangements covering bacon and dairy produce. This system had been modified in various ways by the Conservative Government after 1970 with a view to bringing policy more into line with that of the Six. Even so, the differences between British agricultural policy and the CAP on 1 January 1973 were still considerable. It is not surprising that Mr Joseph Godber, the Minister of Agriculture, quickly found himself in head-on collision with his opposite numbers over food prices under the CAP.

COMMONWEALTH AND CAP

The main commodities of concern to Commonwealth and other

developing countries affected by the CAP were grains (including rice), beef products, fruit and vegetables, including canned fruit, oilseeds and products made from them, and sugar. All these items are protected in broadly the same way under CAP. A system of variable levies is used to make up the difference between world market prices and those fixed by the Community. For cereals the Community sets a target price which is the price producers are intended to receive, on average, for their grain. This target price, which is not in any sense a guaranteed one, comes in between a threshold price below which imports from Commonwealth and other non-member countries cannot enter, and an intervention price at which surpluses will be bought by the Community from budget funds.

The big criticism of the CAP is that it is conducted as a statistical exercise which simply sets the supply of Community agricultural products against their consumption and strikes a balance. A booklet published by the Commission in August 1972, entitled *The Common Agricultural Policy*, stated quite boldly that, 'accession of the four new member countries' (Norway was still a candidate) would make relatively little difference to the supply/demand balance for agricultural products in an enlarged Community. Although Britain is a big net importer of food, Denmark and Ireland are both substantial exporters and taken together the four constitute a fairly balanced unit.' On 1967–8 figures it was reckoned that an enlarged Community would be about eighty-five per cent self-sufficient in the foods which could be grown in Europe. This is a factual statement of the situation, but it makes no reference to higher food prices in the United Kingdom, the switch to a new form of price support which involves closing the British market to foreign suppliers, and the impact of this change on countries which previously relied on exporting foodstuffs to Britain. Nor is there any reference to the considerable cost of CAP to the British balance of payments. It is hard to imagine that a system justified by accountancy and administrative expediency rather than its economic and social effects will long survive its application in a Community of Nine.

THE DILEMMA OF SUGAR

The attitude of the Six to the fall in food imports with the increase in Community self-sufficiency has been to point out that the countries most affected, the United States, Canada and the original EFTA members, were all rich, high-income countries, well able to look after themselves. The relatively small proportion of imports coming from developing countries outside the EEC system made it possible to overlook the difficulties created there. Of all the commodities involved in this trade none has received more attention than sugar. Here the problem was complicated by the fact that sugar production in the Six was covered by CAP, while the Commonwealth Sugar Agreement and other international arrangements regulated trade from other countries. The EEC single-stage market for sugar came into force on 1 July 1968 when a common target price for refined sugar of £93.13 per ton was set for the 1968-9 season. With a level of self-sufficiency of 105 per cent, the EEC was a net exporter of sugar, and producers had a secure market at prices guaranteed at the level of the intervention price of £90.00 per ton. These prices applied in north-east France, the region of greatest surplus, and variations on them applied in other areas. Imports from third countries were protected by a levy designed to bring the world price up to the Community target price. The proceeds of these levies were paid to FEOGA, which had the responsibility of intervening in the market to help meet various storage costs and the subsidization of exports. If the rate of self-sufficiency rose above 135 per cent, producers received no guarantees on either market access or price. With target and intervention prices well above those ruling over recent years, it is not surprising that the EEC sugar system resulted in considerable surpluses.

The obligations of the Commonwealth Sugar Agreement will be continued under the Treaty of Accession until the end of 1974, after which imports from developing Commonwealth countries into the Community would be on the basis of associate membership or a negotiated special trading relationship. The position of India is to be negotiated separately. The countries involved in the Agreement are Antigua, Barbados, Fiji, Guyana, India, Jamaica, Kenya, Mauritius, Swaziland, Trinidad and Tobago, Uganda, St

162

Kitts-Nevis-Anguilla, and Belize. What was the Commonwealth Sugar agreement and how did it operate?

The object of the Commonwealth system was to secure a balance between domestic production of sugar and imports from the Commonwealth, with a margin left over for supplies from other producers. UK domestic beet production was based on a system of maximum acreages to which a guaranteed price applied. Both acreages and prices were determined at the United Kingdom annual price review. The supply of sugar to the market was regulated by the Sugar Board, which sold sugar at the world price, so enabling trade to take place on free market terms. Accounts were adjusted by raising a levy on sugar consumed in the UK or, in the opposite case, making a distribution payment. This arrangement was possible as the UK was the only buyer.

The Commonwealth Sugar Agreement is due to be reviewed at the end of July 1974, when new arrangements allowing for the extension of the European Community will be worked out. These will have to take account not only of the accession of Britain, Denmark and Ireland to the Community but also of the position of the Commonwealth sugar-producing countries, some of which will by then have become associates. The CAP as operated by the Six encouraged domestic production and gave no guarantee of access or of price to cane sugar production except from the French Overseas Departments (DOM) of Réunion, Guadeloupe and Martinique. Associated states received no CAP levy preferences on sugar. What happens to the Commonwealth producers will depend on a number of factors. One is how far the British Government is able to influence Community thinking on agricultural self-sufficiency. The idea that those countries with trade losses on the agricultural roundabouts can make these good on the industrial swings is not an adequate answer for the developing countries. Another factor is the course of the negotiations for association of the various Commonwealth countries. Of the members of the Commonwealth Sugar Agreement, Mauritius applied for associate status in 1972, and Fiji, Jamaica, Barbados, Trinidad and Tobago, Guyana, Kenya, Uganda, Tanzania and Swaziland all have the option of becoming associates. Also Belize, St Kitts, Antigua, St Lucia and St Vincent are all dependencies, whose interests are the responsibility of the British Government. The remaining members are India, a non-associable, and Australia, which was not directly involved in the Community negotiations.

The future arrangements for sugar will also be affected by other sets of negotiations which will take place before the expiry of the Commonwealth Sugar Agreement. The first of these is the International Sugar Agreement due for renegotiation before the end of 1973. This agreement came into operation in 1969 with all the parties to the Commonwealth Sugar Agreement amongst its members. It is a commodity agreement, with production quotas and provision for stock-holding and guarantees of supply to importers. Prices are fixed according to a series of reference points. The Commonwealth producers export part, in some cases the major part, of their output under this agreement. The important question here is whether the Community will be able to play an active part in the operation of the Agreement, an exercise in which the UK could have a decisive role. Also due for renegotiation is the American Sugar Act, which determines imports into the United States. Negotiations for the renewal of the Yaounde Convention, or an agreement replacing it, started in the autumn of 1973 and are due for conclusion by the end of 1974. The original Convention did not include sugar, and attempts by the eighteen Yaounde developing countries to have it included in the 1969 convention failed.

It may be that an augmented group of associates might succeed in bringing sugar into a new Convention. This in itself might help the countries concerned but could leave other Commonwealth producers out on a limb. In this context it is important to recall that the British government promised continuing access for at least 1.4 million tons of Commonwealth sugar at fair prices to the enlarged Community. It has been suggested by the Chairman of the Commonwealth Sugar Exporters Association, Lord Campbell of Eskan,* that sugar negotiations would be better conducted separately from association and trade agreements. Experience of the CAP), where commodities are treated in bulk without regard to any special conditions, certainly lends strength to this view. Although the sugar producers have been fortunate enough to have an effective organization for the marketing of their products it does not follow that they would continue to flourish if this was dis-

* See the Commonwealth Sugar Exporters' Association Annual Review, 1972.

mantled and set up in a different way. While it is possible that the sugar producers among the Yaounde countries together with the four African members of the Commonwealth Sugar Agreement might be fitted into an arrangement that gave them a reasonable return, it is extremely unlikely that the rest of the Commonwealth producers would be able to maintain their position if dealt with on a piecemeal basis.

SOLUTIONS FOR DEVELOPING COUNTRIES

The problem posed by the enlargement of the European Community for the developing countries of the Commonwealth as producers of primary products can be treated in one of two ways. The first is to safeguard their interests by what in effect would be Community commodity agreements related to the CAP. The second would be for the Community and its associates to take part in international commodity agreements. The first solution would be costly for the Nine as, if operated on CAP lines, it would involve intervention prices and subsidies, not to mention the nightmare of surpluses. The world market, as the experience of the sugar producers has shown, is a residual market able to absorb a limited tonnage over and above the requirements met through normal trading channels. It would be easy enough to produce an extra 1.4 million tons of sugar in the enlarged Community rather than import this amount from the Commonwealth. The effect of such a loss on the developing countries would not be offset by any boosting of Community aid programmes.

OILSEEDS TOO

What has been said of sugar is even more true in the case of oilseeds, the producers of which do not have the advantage of an efficient central marketing organization. Here the main suppliers of the UK market are Nigeria, The Gambia and Malawi among the potential associates, and India and Malaysia among the non-associables. The main problem is that associates will receive preferential duty-free entry while non-associables will lose their Commonwealth preference and begin to pay a levy on their exports to Britain as a Community member.

For the non-associables, British membership of the European Community has a number of serious consequences. Malaysia for example will lose Commonwealth Preferences for its exports of palm oil and coconut oil, and for such exports as canned pineapple, in four stages up to 1 July 1977. The introduction of the common external tariff on imports into Britain, by stages from January 1974, means that these products become dutiable in the British market. A more general effect would be the fact that associated countries in Africa and the Caribbean would enjoy preferential treatment in the Community including the United Kingdom. Exports from Malaysia and other non-associables would therefore be at a double disadvantage in the United Kingdom, where they were previously enjoying a preference. In the case of palm oil from Malaysia, imports formerly entered the UK market duty-free while those from non-Commonwealth sources paid a duty of ten per cent. As the duty on palm oil in the Community is six per cent, Malaysian exports will have a net tariff loss of sixteen per cent by the time preferences have been phased out and the common external tariff phased in. To the rest of the Community exporting over a six per cent tariff will not be too difficult, and indeed exports rose in the years before enlargement.

This should not disguise the fact that Malaysia and other non-associables will be considerably worse off in total because of their losses in the UK market, which took some $57m. worth of Malaysia's palm oil in 1970. The situation is made worse by the existence of plans to expand palm oil exports under Malaysian Federal Land Development Authority schemes. These plans, due to mature in 1975, are forecast to raise palm oil exports to about 1,250,000 tons compared with 394,000 tons in 1970. The problems posed by palm oil, and to a lesser extent by canned pineapple and coconut oil, are very real to a country like Malaysia. These products are not covered by commodity agreements and are unlikely to be so in the future. What emerges from this example is the fact that discrimination in favour of associates may promote development in one area but bring depression to another. When both are members of the Commonwealth the situation becomes even more confused.

COMMODITY AGREEMENTS

In the past, the Six have acted independently in relation to international commodity agreements. Some have joined, some have not, and there has been no move to impose uniformity on a Community basis. All of the Six are members of the Fourth International Tin Agreement and the EEC has the status of an associate observer member. This has not prevented the individual countries from following an independent line, and the Netherlands and France were in fact the only consumer countries contributing to the fund to finance the Tin Agreement buffer stock. The EEC is a full participating member of the International Wheat Agreement and its membership reflects the need for coordinated action imposed by the requirements of CAP. For sugar the situation is equally clear but from the opposite point of view. The EEC is not a member of the International Sugar Agreement, as in this case the CAP requirement is on the side of the sugar beet producers and against the more numerous and highly vulnerable cane sugar exporters.

In general the Six are less dependent on imports for their supplies of primary commodities than are Britain or Japan. This greater self-sufficiency, which links up with the thinking behind the CAP, is one of the main reasons why the Community has not taken a leading part in promoting any of the international commodity agreements. If the urge to self-sufficiency should spread to the United Kingdom the prospects for the traditional suppliers of primary products from the Commonwealth countries would be depressing indeed. Trade in agricultural commodities and their production in the Community are two aspects of the same activity. What matters is the actual size of the agricultural industry in the enlarged Community rather than whether production is subsidized by the CAP system or by UK deficiency payments. When some clear answer to this key question has been arrived at, it should be possible for the Community to consider its position in relation to commodity agreements. The emphasis in this field is now less on the use of agreements to stabilize prices and more on their value as a means of promoting activity and generating employment. Agreement is needed to incorporate all commodity schemes into a general programme covering trade and development which will enable developing countries to maintain or increase their earnings

167

of foreign exchange while implementing plans to diversify their economies. This is an area in which the Community could take a leading part, provided the requirements of the CAP and of the developing countries, especially the non-associables, can be seen in the right perspective.

12. Next Steps Forward

GLOBAL CONSIDERATIONS

This book has been concerned with the effect of the creation of the enlarged Community on international economic relations. Setting up the Common Market of the Six necessitated trading agreements with the former colonies of the member countries, and the placing of former national arrangements for external trade onto a Community basis. Enlargement of the Community has necessitated the extension of this process not only to the three new members but through the United Kingdom to the Commonwealth countries. Because of the importance of the Nine and their place in world trade and finance, the mere existence of an organization in which they are banded together with common aims affects the rest of the world. For the industrialized countries it has necessitated a reconsideration of the Bretton Woods system. For the developing countries the impact of the enlarged Community could be as great for those not associated in any way as for the favoured countries granted preferential access to the Common Market.

At international level, the Community is basically a regional grouping, but because of its association with countries in the Mediterranean, Africa and elsewhere it inevitably affects the operation of the international institutions of the United Nations and World Bank groups. This process raises questions for which no answers can be given without further experience of the operation of the Community. Over the last two decades the world has been moving slowly and sometimes painfully towards non-discrimination and the removal of obstacles to free trade, and a more rational system of international payments. At the same time through the DAC the industrialized countries have been attempting to organize the flow of assistance from them to the developing countries. No one knows whether progress on these three fronts – trade, monetary arrangements and aid and technical assistance – will be faster or slower because of the creation of the enlarged Community in Europe. The three UNCTAD Conferences 1964, 1968 and 1972, have shown that there is considerable dissatisfaction among the developing countries regarding the operation of the global institutions and their own rate of progress towards development.

It is possible to argue that enlargement of the Community undermines the whole framework of non-discrimination on which the world trading and monetary systems have been built up. If the process was carried farther the fragmentation of the world economy could become a reality. It is possible to imagine the Pacific area growing rapidly in economic terms, focused on Japan. This could have a counterpart in a North American region with particular concern for Latin America and the Caribbean. Across the Atlantic the enlarged Community with its special interests in the Mediterranean and Africa already exists. The integration of the economies of the USSR and the COMECON countries has been a political and economic factor since the ending of the Second World War. The emergence of China as a major world power raises, in spite of her membership of the United Nations, the prospect that a very considerable part of the world's surface and population will be outside the institutional framework of the world economy for some considerable time to come. Yet another regional grouping could be possible in the Middle East, where the logic of the world energy shortage has become clear to the rulers of the Arabian Gulf States. Their importance in the world economy is due not simply to the fact that they now contain between them some fifty-five per cent of the world's oil reserves, which by the end of the 1970s may be around seventy-five per cent, but that as a result of this they have control over an increasing proportion of the world's convertible currencies. By contrast with this wealthy regional group there is the problem of the Indian subcontinent, too big to be assimilated in any other group, too poor to operate alone.

A subdivision of the world into regional groups on these lines is already more than an outside possibility. Its political implications need to be clearly examined. The object of the Schuman Plan was to make war in Europe impossible for the future. Setting up the Community would appear to have achieved this object. It could hardly be counted as progress however if outlawing war at national level created the possibility that it might take place at some indeterminate time in the future at regional or continental level. Another possibility is that the formation of regional blocs would generate protectionist attitudes. The United States might decide to turn in on itself and use its enormous industrial power to increase its level of self-sufficiency. On the other hand the Americans might feel that it was more important to maintain their position in the world and the only way to do this would be to step up aid to countries in the Pacific region as a counter to Japanese influence.

COMMUNITY EXTERNAL RELATIONS

The Community system, if adopted by each of the continents of the world, would clearly mean the end of the move towards a multi-lateral world trading system. The fact such a development might take place underlines the importance of the external relations of the Community with the United States, Japan and the Soviet Bloc. In this connection the magnitude of the European operation is such that most Community activities produce a reaction from non-member countries. This is particularly true with regard to CAP and the discriminatory trade agreements made by the Community. To say this immediately raises the question whether the Community, in its enlarged form, is an enormous mistake. Is it permissible to have a customs union on the scale of Benelux or CARIFTA but not one containing 250 million people organized in a wealthy industrial society? This is a question that can only be answered in the light of experience. Organizing industry to enable maximum advantage to be taken of modern technology requires large-scale units and access to mass markets. From this point of view, the only way in which the Nine could maintain a competitive position against the United States and Japan was through combining their resources. The tremendous growth in world trade during the 1960s has been largely the result of trade liberalization through the removal of tariffs and quotas. At the same time lower tariffs mean the erosion of preferences. This could be taken to mean that discrimination at regional level was being offset by action taken by the same countries at global level.

171

Another question for which no immediate answers are possible is whether non-discrimination is in fact the best policy in all cases. Would the developing countries be better off if the Yaounde Agreement had never been signed or the Commonwealth Preference System had not evolved? The answer depends entirely on the position of the respondent. Those not benefiting from a preferential arrangement can see the advantages much more clearly than those who do. In a world where there are not enough cakes and ale for everyone, should we spend our time ensuring that no one gets either? If non-discrimination is to be adopted as the working principle for the conduct of international trade it must produce tangible results for a sufficiently large proportion of the world's peoples. It has been argued in UNCTAD and elsewhere that the principle of non-discrimination has relevance mainly to the needs of the rich industrialized countries and is not appropriate for the developing countries.

In an imperfect world, the preparation of ideal blueprints can be a self-defeating exercise. Raising the living standards of the peoples of the developing countries depends on a better use of the world's resources and the creation of more wealth to share. It is here that the great importance of the Community in the world economy lies. Higher rates of economic growth in Europe must be translated in terms of increased resources. What happens to these resources, how are they used by and for the Nine, and how do they influence development elsewhere? The objections to the formation of regional groups are only valid if these result in a world economy broken up into half a dozen separate, exclusive, and potentially antagonistic blocs. The object of the external policies of the European Community must be to prevent such a situation from developing.

LOOKING OUTWARDS

So far as world peace is concerned, the major issues will continue to depend on the relations between the super-powers. In this context the role of the European Community is limited but nevertheless of critical importance. The position, size, and dense population of Western Europe make it extremely vulnerable in a nuclear age. While Europe must be in a position to defend itself – and here it is to be hoped that the unsatisfactory situation in NATO will soon be resolved – the Community should not become a military super-power itself. The importance of the Community in world affairs must depend on its economic strength exercised through its role in world trade. For this role to be sustained it will be necessary for the Community to develop satisfactory relationships with both Eastern Europe and the United States. These will only be possible if the interests of all three are compatible with the objectives of Japan, the other major industrial power, and the developing countries.

The relationship between the Community and the United States has changed considerably during the 1960s. To some extent this has arisen from a growing impatience over the slowness of the Community to assume a more significant role in maintaining the world's monetary system. Equally important is the wave of questioning that has been brought about in the United States by the war in Vietnam and by a diminishing confidence in the ability of America to influence the course of events in other parts of the world. Failure to solve specific domestic problems and questions about the operation of the political system are other factors in the situation. While there is considerable uncertainty about the sort of external policies that the United States should pursue, some clearly defined attitudes are discernible.* One strongly-held view is that the United States should itself be less active abroad and should look to other nations to shoulder a greater share of responsi-bility. This question leads on to asking why the United States should play any substantial foreign role at all and what its essen-tial interests abroad are. What should be American trade and mone-tary policies in a changing economic and political environment? There is considerably more agreement on the need for change than there is on the form that it should take.

A number of common themes and conclusions can be dis-cerned. The first of these is that emphasis in American foreign policy should move away from its preoccupation with East–West relationships and concentrate on economic and other problems within the non-Communist world. Another is that the main indus-trial areas – the United States, the European Community and

* See *The Next Phase in Foreign Policy*, ed. Henry Owen, the Brookings Institution, Washington April 1973.

Japan – should work out joint approaches to world problems which in the past have been tackled largely by the United States acting alone. The third element is a disenchantemnt with the concept of the American security role in the developing world and of the utility of force to advance long-term US interests. Each of these themes is relevant to the consideration of the role of the European Community in the world economy. However it is the second theme, the possibility of joint US, Community and Japanese cooperation, that has the greatest immediate importance. This assumes that the main problems in the 1970s will be found in the economic sphere. Success in solving them will require a considerable effort by the Community and Japan in assuming new responsibilities and by the Americans in agreeing to relinquish existing ones. A move towards increased reliance on multilateral operations, in which American influence was less than in the past, would not necessarily satisfy the new trend in American public opinion. The most hopeful sign is perhaps the fact that opinion in the United States is no longer formed in the images created by the influence of cold war coalitions and the decline in the powers of the European nation states. In this situation, provided the administration is able to sustain an acceptable position, the spending reforms of the IMF and in GATT are important.

Looking to the East, the European Community's relationships with the Soviet Union have been slow to develop in any formal manner. The Soviet government has refused to have any official dealings with the Community, and other East European states have necessarily fallen into line. This position has now changed, and although some ambiguities remain, relationships between the Community and the COMECON states have now been established and are beginning to operate in the context of trade agreements. The suspicion that the European Community was an instrument invented by the Americans as a means of setting up a united front against the East appears to be less strongly held than it was. Certainly the suspicions and doubts were not entirely without foundation. The Community has served as a framework within which it has been possible for the Federal Republic to rebuild its economic strength. However the way in which the Community has developed in the late 1960s and the growing sharpness in its dealings with the United States has reduced the idea that it was a

174

tool of American diplomacy to the level of dogma.

Relationships with the Soviet Union are necessarily affected by the fact that its foreign trade is a marginal activity accounting at most for two to three per cent of its national product. This is not the case with the COMECON countries, which depend in varying degrees on foreign markets as outlets for their industrial goods and agricultural products. The COMECON states also look to the West for new technology and the sophisticated products needed to maintain it. For this reason they are likely to make increasing use of partnerships with enterprises in the West as the means of enabling them to establish new industries utilizing technologies in which they were previously not proficient. The partial successes achieved by Herr Brandt in securing a closer relationship with the USSR and easing the tension between East and West Germany may be essential first steps towards securing better relations between the Community and the Eastern Bloc. This must be looked at in conjunction with the possibility that the United States will begin to withdraw from the active defence of Western Europe, leaving the Community if not to its own devices, certainly responsible for its security. In any case the Community will continue to be in a situation where the big decisions settling the essential military and strategic framework of international relations are likely to be made by the Americans and the Russians. For the first decade of its existence the Community flourished under the American umbrella, without the need for any coherent foreign policy of its own. In the 1970s the international environment is likely to be less friendly, with the result that the Community will have to press forward towards political integration at a faster rate. The alternative to this would be disengagement by the member states, with Britain leading the rush to the exit.

The other main aspect of the Community's external relations centres on the Mediterranean and Africa. This concentration has largely been thrust upon the Community by history, tradition and the facts of geography. When the Rome Treaty was signed, France was engaged in a war with Algeria, its last colonial war, and the French African colonies were still some years away from independence. One of the main reasons why President de Gaulle was unwilling to accommodate the Commonwealth at the time of the Macmillan negotiations for entry to the Common Market was that it was already encumbered with Francophone states. Because the Community has taken its cue from France, the major ex-colonial power of the original six members, it has excluded Asia and to a lesser extent Latin America from its external policies. The fact that the member states have bilateral aid policies and these operate in countries outside the Community orbit does not prevent the developing countries from taking the view that the Community is pro-African. The arrival of a large group of Commonwealth African countries as potential associates of the Community has consolidated the concept of Eurafrica as a major feature of Community external relations.

The fact that the Community has used its ties with the developing countries to build up a series of special relationships contained in association agreements is another aspect of the position which is not favourably regarded by developing countries generally, nor indeed by some of the actual and potential associates. The Community has not made a good showing in the UNCTAD Conferences and it may be said that the individual member states have had to devise their own policies on the main issues affecting the developing countries. In this connection the truth of the matter lies to some extent in the fact that the Community has been developing in a changing world. The need to prevent war between the individual European countries, the original driving force of the Schuman Plan, no longer applies. As Barbara Ward has said, 'the great fault lines of world society do not now lie chiefly down the Rhine. The coming eruptions of history are beginning their seismic disturbance in other continents and along other lines of weakness. A division which was virtually unheard of when the Treaty of Rome was signed – the division between the developed, industrial 'North' of our planet, and the developing 'South' – is beginning to move towards the centre of the world's agenda of survival.'*

PROSPECTS AND OPPORTUNITIES

Perhaps the most important fact to realize about the European Community is that it is essentially an old-fashioned concept. There

* E. Pearse and R. Kahn, *The White Tribes of Europe* Action for World Development and Churches Action for World Development, November 1970. Introduction by Barbara Ward.

has been a great deal of talk about the need for Britain to adapt its practices and procedures to those of the Community, and we have come to believe that in our insular state we have fallen behind the continentals and must now throw overboard our old ideas and beliefs and take up those of the Six. Nothing could in fact be farther from the truth. The justification for uniting Europe does not depend on the annoying trivia of integration, such as the adoption of the decimal and metric systems. The European Community and British membership of it would be a worthwhile venture to the extent, not simply that they contribute to the solution of European problems, but that they place their solution in a workable context.

Negotiations between Britain and the Six were not concerned only with the national interests of each of the member countries. Overseas trade and the economic and social development of Africa, Asia, Latin America are all affected by them. But it would be wrong to overemphasize the importance of increasing the wealth of the Community in order to raise the flow of resources to the developing countries. This is one aspect of Community external relations, but by no means the most important. British entry into the Common Market is basically a political decision. It assumes that an eventual partnership of equals between an enlarged Community and the United States could be a major contribution to the solution of world problems. By contrast it accepts that it is no longer possible for the United Kingdom to uphold 'special' relationships with the Commonwealth, the United States and the Community of the Six as an individual nation state.

The decision taken by Mr Heath's government reflects the view that Britain can make a greater contribution to world problems within the broader framework of the Community than operating on a different and sometimes competing wavelength outside. Economic integration and the advantages of a mass market with its counterpart of advanced technology clearly offer advantages which a go-it-alone policy would not provide. However, simply to bring nine nations with their varying resources and aspirations together does not by itself solve any problems or indeed bring solutions any nearer. It would after all be possible to procure agreement on the kind of general objectives set out in the Treaty of Accession by a straightforward international agreement between governments. What makes the Community different is the fact that it was based on major political commitments which themselves arose from a basis of historical circumstances and the experience of dealing with common problems in similar ways. Acceptance of the Community entails recognizing the fact that a separate British policy based on the Commonwealth is no longer tenable. This does not mean a rejection of the Commonwealth but rather that its objectives must now be pursued by other means.

To say therefore that the Community is an old-fashioned concept is simply to recognize that it is based on an ideal that has now been overtaken by events. The fact that this ideal, the prevention of future wars between the West European states, is common to all the Community countries represents a starting point. The Community becomes an organization committed to the search for alternatives. It provides its members with the resources, but not yet the political means, to extend the influence of Europe throughout the world economy to an extent which in the past could only be accomplished by war.

The spread of Community influence will depend on creating strong political institutions able to translate national opinions and objectives into Community policies. At the present time, except for relatively simple problems, Community decision-making has not been remarkable for speed or clarity. Important subjects are still decided by horse-trading involving the national interests of the member states. This process is likely to continue for the foreseeable future, and it may be well into the 1980s before the process of political integration has proceeded far enough to produce Community institutions capable of taking decisions on a European basis. In the meantime the Community has to find its way about in a changing world and decide on its position in relation to the United States, USSR, Japan and the developing countries. At the same time the role of the global institutions has to be redefined in terms of the 1970s rather than those of the years immediately following the Second World War.

It may be that it would take ten or fifteen years for the Community to develop decision-making institutions able to satisfy national ambitions. These institutions after all are not instruments designed to carry out a clear-cut common purpose in a preordained manner, but rather the expression of national objectives taken in constantly changing circumstances. Because the external rela-

178

tionships of the Community will be increasingly important over the next decade, the pressure to create institutions capable of dealing with the problems involved will be maintained. In other words, having created a Community in the image of the first half of the twentieth century the Nine now have to adapt this to meet the problems and tasks of the second half. The pressures for this adaptation will come increasingly from outside the Community, on the principle that great economic power carries with it commensurate responsibilities.

THE STARTING POINT

So far the Community has not applied itself to the problems of the world economy. The big opportunity to start doing so is provided by the GATT negotiations which began in September 1973. These talks, which will be concerned not only with the technical problems of trade liberalization but also with the relationships between the various trading groups of the developed nations and the Third World, represent an opportunity for the Community to negotiate with the United States and Japan regarding the trade in industrial products and foodstuffs and raw materials. They will take place not against a background of endless resources awaiting development but in a situation where economic growth has to be balanced by environmental considerations and the growing scarcity of raw materials and energy sources. The negotiations are also unique in that for the first time the developing countries will be stating their case for the right to an increased share of world trade.

The GATT negotiations will no doubt demonstrate that in some ways the enlargement of the Community has complicated the work of international organizations, and certainly from the British point of view negotiating at second hand through Community spokesmen will not come easily. While agreement on a common position between the Nine is a necessary preliminary to a successful negotiation, the Community has so far not been too successful at doing this, as for example in the UNCTAD conferences, where its participation has been impaired by failure to reach agreement between the Six. The development of common policies in the international field will not be easy, and it will take time for the peoples of the individual member states to become reconciled

179

to the surrender of sovereignty that the new situation requires. It is to be hoped therefore that in the GATT negotiations the Nine will concentrate on matters on which they can agree, where their bargaining power can be used to maximum effect.

It remains to be seen whether the nine-nation Community with its increased economic power in relation to the United States will be able to use its strength wisely. The whole point about British membership is that it should be able to contribute to international policy-making in a way that will spread Community influence over a wider range of problems. This does not mean that Britain will be attempting to turn the Community into a different sort of organization, or that she is still hankering after a free trade area rather than an integrated Community. The fact that Britain's interests traditionally lie outside Europe should be the means of turning Community attention in outward directions. Outside the Community, Britain would have had little hope of success in such an objective. Inside, it may be able to help its members to give an international expression to the external policies of the Community.

Epilogue

1973 will be remembered as the year when the Six at last managed to agree to admit the United Kingdom to the European Community and faced up to the responsibilities that go with economic power. Dr Henry Kissinger has called it the 'year of Europe' and has talked of a new Atlantic Charter. The problems of the Nixon administration, with the accompanying setback to American leadership of the non-communist world, have changed the emphasis in European–US relations.

However the emergence of new problems does not remove the necessity of dealing with existing ones. What are the problems on the agenda involving the external relations of the European Community? They can be listed briefly as follows:

1 Creating a new world monetary system that takes account of the changes of the past twenty years and that will replace the ambiguous mixture of fixed and adjustable parities that has existed since the American decisions of 15 August 1971.
2 Updating the world trading system based on the GATT rules.
3 Reforming the arrangements for trade in agricultural products with special reference to the protectionist features of the CAP.
4 Reconsidering the problems of the Third World in terms of trade, aid and payments, and the ways in which these are dealt with by the global institutions.
5 European defence and its connection with the evolution of the European Community towards political integration.
6 The continuing difficulties experienced in relation to trade and investment in the Japanese market.

In the European Community there is no mechanism for dealing with these problems. For the GATT talks a common negotiating

181

position was possible, based on a compromise between the interests of the member states. It would be true to say that the preparatory internal discussions presented more difficulties than the negotiations themselves. In the monetary sphere the Community countries have given themselves until 1980 to work out a common policy. In the meantime they have been unable to agree on a Community float.

What has happened so far is that the Nine have pooled their good intentions. For the moment these are not enough to bring the political influence of the Community up to the level of its economic strength – the unwritten item on the agenda of world problems. In terms of achievement, the Six have formed a customs union, introduced a common agricultural policy and agreed to admit three new members to their charmed circle. This is still a long way from having a European Community that is able to take a leading part in shaping the future of the world economy. Can the Nine achieve what the Six have failed to do? Can Britain exert the sort of influence that will make the Community into something more than a pyramid of associate members? This is the heart of the matter. This is what European unity is all about.

Appendix 1. The European Community

1 Six original members:
   France   W. Germany   Italy
   Holland   Belgium   Luxembourg
2 Three new members:
   United Kingdom   Denmark   Ireland
3 Associates in Europe:
   Greece   Turkey   Spain
4 Former EFTA countries with free trade treaties with Community:
   Austria   Switzerland
   Sweden   Norway   Iceland   Portugal
   Finland
5 Mediterranean countries with preferential trade agreements with Community:
   Israel   Malta   Morocco   Tunisia   Egypt
   Spain   Cyprus   Lebanon   Jordan   Algeria
   Yugoslavia
6 Yaounde Convention countries:

Burundi	Dahomey	Niger
Cameroon	Gabon	Rwanda
Central African	Ivory Coast	Senegal
Republic	Madagascar	Somalia
Chad	Mali	Togo
Congo-Brazzaville	Mauritania	Upper Volta
		Zaire

7 Commonwealth countries with option of joining Yaounde Convention, Arusha Convention or negotiating special trading agreements:
   Kenya   Uganda   Tanzania (existing signatories of
                         Arusha Convention)
   Botswana   Nigeria   Sierra Leone

Swaziland   Zambia   Malawi
Barbados   Guyana   Jamaica Trinidad and Tobago
Fiji   Tonga   Western Samoa
Mauritius (applied to participate in Yaounde Convention 29 July 1969)
The Gambia   Lesotho   Ghana

8 Dependent territories of the United Kingdom:

Bahamas*	Gilbert and Ellice Islands Colony
Bermuda	Montserrat
British Antarctic Territory	New Hebrides
British Honduras	Pitcairn
British Indian Ocean Territory	St Helena and Dependencies
British Solomon Island Protectorate	Seychelles
British Virgin Islands	Turks and Caicos Islands
Brunei	West Indian Associated
Cayman Islands	States (Antigua,
Central and Southern Line Islands	Dominica, Grenada, St Lucia, St Vincent, St
Falkland Islands and Dependencies	Kitts, Nevis, Anguilla)

9 European territories included in the customs territory of the European Community:
Gibraltar   Channel Islands

10 Overseas Departments of France (DOM):
Guadeloupe   Guyane   Martinique   Réunion

11 Overseas Territories of France (TOM):
St Pierre et Miquelon   French Somaliland
Comores   New Caledonia   Wallis and Futuna
French Oceania   New Hebrides
Antarctic Territories

12 Overseas Territories of the Netherlands:
Netherlands Antilles

13 Overseas Territories of Denmark:
Faroe Islands   Greenland

* The Bahamas became independent on 10 July 1973 and may opt for association.

184

Appendix 2. European Community Generalized Preference Scheme

As a general rule manufactured and semi-manufactured goods from the following countries will enter the European Community duty-free.

Afghanistan	Dominican	Malagasy Republic
Algeria	Republic	Malaysia
Arab Republic	El Salvador	Maldives
of Egypt	Ecuador	Mali
Saudi Arabia	Ethiopia	Mauritania
Argentina	Gabon	Mauritius
Bangladesh	Gambia	Mexico
Barbados	Ghana	Morocco
Burma	Guatemala	Nepal
Bolivia	Guinea	Nicaragua
Botswana	Haiti	Niger
Brazil	Honduras	Nigeria
Burundi	India	Pakistan
Cambodia	Indonesia	Panama
Cameroun	Irak	Paraguay
Central African	Ivory Coast	Peru
Republic	Jamaica	The Philippines
Chad	Jordan	Rwanda
Chile	Kenya	Senegal
Cyprus	Kuwait	Sierra Leone
Colombia	Laos	Singapore
Congo-	Lebanon	Somalia
Brazzaville	Lesotho	Sri Lanka
Costa Rica	Liberia	Swaziland
Dahomey	Libya	Sudan

Syria	Tunisia	Yemen
Tanzania	Uganda	South Yemen
Thailand	Upper Volta	Yugoslavia
Togo	Uruguay	Zaire
Trinidad and	Venezuela	Zambia
Tobago	Vietnam	Romania

The system also applies to certain 'dependent territories,' including Spanish North Africa, Portuguese Guinea, Angola, Mozambique, British Honduras, the Bahamas, the Bermudas, Timor, Macao, Pacific Islands administered by the US, British Oceania and West Indies. In addition to the above, Hong Kong will benefit from the Community's plan but with the exclusion of textiles and shoes. Still under consideration are Israel, Spain, Turkey, Greece and Malta, with all of which countries the Community already has preferential arrangements of various kinds. Portugal and Taiwan may also be included.

Appendix 3. Declaration of Commonwealth Principles

Agreed by Commonwealth Heads of Government meeting at Singapore, 22 January 1971

The Commonwealth of Nations is a voluntary association of independent sovereign States, each responsible for its own policies, consulting and co-operating in the common interests of their peoples and in the promotion of international understanding and world peace.

Members of the Commonwealth come from territories in the six continents and five oceans, include peoples of different races, languages and religions, and display every stage of economic development from poor developing nations to wealthy industrialized nations. They encompass a rich variety of cultures, traditions and institutions.

Membership of the Commonwealth is compatible with the freedom of member-Governments to be non-aligned or to belong to any other grouping, association or alliance. Within this diversity all members of the Commonwealth hold certain principles in common. It is by pursuing these principles that the Commonwealth can continue to influence international society for the benefit of mankind.

We believe that international peace and order are essential to the security and prosperity of mankind; we therefore support the United Nations and seek to strengthen its influence for peace in the world, and its efforts to remove the causes of tension between nations.

We believe in the liberty of the individual, in equal rights for all citizens regardless of race, colour, creed or political belief, and in their inalienable right to participate by means of free and democratic political processes in framing the society in which they live.

We therefore strive to promote in each of our countries those representative institution and guarantees for personal freedom under the law that are out common heritage.

We recognize racial prejudice as a dangerous sickness threatening the healthy development of the human race and racial discrimination as an unmitigated evil of society. Each of us will vigorously combat this evil within our own nation.

No country will afford to regimes which practise racial discrimination assistance which in its own judgment directly contributes to the pursuit or consolidation of this evil policy. We oppose all forms of colonial domination and racial oppression and are committed to the principles of human dignity and equality.

We will therefore use all our efforts to foster human equality and dignity everywhere, and to further the principles of self-determination and non-racialism.

We believe that the wide disparities in wealth now existing between different sections of mankind are too great to be tolerated. They also create world tensions. Our aim is their progressive removal. We therefore seek to use our efforts to overcome poverty, ignorance and disease, in raising standards of life and achieving a more equitable international society.

To this end our aim is to achieve the freest possible flow of international trade) on terms fair and equitable to all, taking into account the special requirements of the developing countries, and to encourage the flow of adequate resources, including governmental and private resources, to the developing countries, bearing in mind the importance of doing this in a true spirit of partnership and of establishing for this purpose in the developing countries conditions which are conducive to sustained investment and growth.

We believe that international co-operation is essential to remove the causes of war, promote tolerance, combat injustice, and secure development among the peoples of the world. We are convinced that the Commonwealth is one of the most fruitful associations for these purposes.

In pursuing these principles the members of the Commonwealth believe that they can provide a constructive example of the multi-national approach which is vital to peace and progress in the modern world. The association is based on consultation, discussion and co-operation.

In rejecting coercion as an instrument of policy they recognize that the security of each member-State from external aggression is a matter of concern to all members. It provides many channels for continuing exchanges of knowledge and views on professional, cultural, economic, legal and political issues among member-States.

These relationships we intend to foster and extend, for we believe that our multi-national association can expand human understanding and understanding among nations, assist in the elimination of discrimination based on differences of race, colour or creed, maintain and strengthen personal liberty, contribute to the enrichment of life for all, and provide a powerful influence for peace among nations.

Bibliography

1 General Works
   The United Kingdom and the European Communities, HMSO,
   Cmnd. 4715, 1971.
   Britain and Europe, CBI, 1967.
   Britain in Europe, a second industrial appraisal, CBI, 1970.
   *Engineering Companies: a study of the impact of UK entry on
   engineering companies, particularly from the standpoint of
   mechanical engineering*, British Mechanical Engineering Con-
   federation in association with *Engineering*, July 1971.
   *Treaty Setting up the European Economic Community and Con-
   nected Documents* (Treaty of Rome), HMSO, 1957.
   *Britain and the European Communities – An Economic Assess-
   ment*, Cmnd. 4289, February 1970.
   *The Common Agricultural Policy of the European Economic
   Community*, Cmnd. 3274, 1967.

2 Trade Problems
   *Towards an Open World Economy; A Trade Policy Research
   Centre Report*, ed. Frank McFadzean, Macmillan, 1972.
   Non-tariff distortions of international trade, Robert E. Baldwin,
   Brookings Institution, George Allen and Unwin, 1970.
   The Structure and Development of the Common Market, A. E.
   Walsh and John Paxton, Hutchinson Ed., 1972.

3 The Developing Countries
   The Frontiers of Development Studies, Paul Streeton, Macmillan, 1972.
   Dissent on Development, P. T. Bauer, Weidenfeld and Nicolson,
   1971.

190

Africa and the Common Market, P. N. C. Okigbo, Longmans, 1969.

The Economics of the Common Market, D. Swann, Penguin Ed., 1972.

Europe: Journey to an Unknown Destination, Andrew Shonfield, Penguin, 1973.

The Seven Outside, Peter Tulloch, Overseas Development Institute, 1973.

Britain the EEC *and the Third World*, Lord Campbell of Eskan and Others, Overseas Development Institute, 1971.

Guidelines for International Investment, International Chamber of Commerce, 1973.

Programme for the Liberalization of International Trade, International Chamber of Commerce, 1971.

The European Communities, A Businessman's A–Z, London Chamber of Commerce, 1972.

Europe and the Developing World, Sir William Gorell Barnes, PEP, 1967.

The United States in a Changing World Economy, vol. 1, A Foreign Economic Perspective, Peter G. Peterson, British-North American Research Association, London, February 1972.

Businessman's Guide to the Common Market, D. Prag and E. D. Nicholson, Pall Mall, April 1973.

4 Official Documents
Convention Establishing the European Free Trade Association (The Stockholm Convention), HMSO, Cmnd. 1026, July 1960.

United States International Economic Policy in an Interdependent World (The Williams Report), US Government, Washington, July 1971.

Index

Geneva, 19, 20, 58, 170
Germany, 105, 107, 108, 119, 130, 131
  see also East Germany *and* West
  Germany
GFR *see* West Germany
Ghana, 44, 52
Gibraltar, 50, 54
Gilbert and Ellis Islands, 52
GNP, 24, 110, 111, 116
Godber, Joseph, 160
grains *see* cereals
Great Britain *see* Britain
Greece, 15, 29–31, 44, 45, 49
Grenada, 52
Gross National Product *see* GNP
groundnuts, 43, 99, 100, 101
Group of Seventy-Seven, 51
Group of Ten, 66
GSP, 54, 82–9, 92, 99, 103, 111, 152,
  154, 158, 185–6
Guadeloupe, 39, 163
Guiana, 39
Guinea, 34, 37
Guyana, 52, 162, 163

Hague, The, 16
Hallstein, Walter, 49
Heath, Edward, 61–2, 131, 177
Hong Kong, 50, 52, 54, 84, 87, 89, 93,
  158
Hungary, 133, 135, 136, 137, 139
hydrocarbon oils, 83

ICC *see* International Chamber of
  Commerce
Iceland, 20, 22, 24, 26, 27, 28
IMF, 11, 14, 59, 60, 66, 80, 103, 130,
  152, 174
India, 14, 16, 17, 50, 51, 54, 60, 80,
  84, 85, 88, 89, 90, 108, 109, 152,
  158, 162, 164, 165, 170
Indian Ocean countries, 50–2, 82, 100
  see also specific countries
industrialization, 89–94, 139, 152–4
Industrial policy in the Community,
  1970 (*Collona Report*), 115
industry, 14, 22, 49, 106, 114, 116,
  154, 171
  see also products, industrial *and*
  tariffs, industrial
International Chamber of Commerce,
  127

International Monetary Fund *see*
  IMF
International Sugar Agreement, 164,
  167
International Tin Agreement
  (Fourth), 167
International Wheat Agreement, 167
Iran, 89
Ireland, 10, 25, 31, 48, 58, 59, 62, 105,
  160, 161, 163
iron, 73
Isle of Man, 62
Israel, 44, 46–7, 48, 49, 89, 147
Italy, 34, 44, 49, 107, 108
Ivory Coast, 34, 37, 96

Jamaica, 52, 84, 162, 163
Japan, 17, 36, 58, 67, 76, 78, 85, 108,
  115, 116, 129, 130, 151, 167, 173,
  174, 178, 179, 181
  Australia and, 73, 75, 81
  East European trade, 138, 139
  fuel supplies and, 142, 146, 147,
  149
  regional importance of, 51, 72, 80,
  170, 171
Jordan, 44
*Journel officiel des Communautés
  Européennes,* 88
Jugoslavia *see* Yugoslavia
jute, 26, 83, 85, 158, 159

Kama Lorry Project, 137
Kennedy Round, 13, 57, 117, 134
Kenya, 43, 52, 98, 111, 162, 163
  see also Arusha Convention
Kissinger, Henry, 181
Korea, Republic of, 88, 89
Korea, South *see* South Korea
Krohn, H. B., 157

labour, 45, 69, 91, 93, 115, 153
Lagos Association Treaty, 44
Lagos Convention (1966), 43–4, 107,
  111
Latin America, 14, 42, 80, 83, 85,
  170, 176, 177
  see also specific countries
lead, 67
leather goods, 83, 89, 158
Lebanon, 44, 47
Lesotho, 52

For Product Safety Concerns and Information please contact our
EU representative GPSR@taylorandfrancis.com Taylor & Francis
Verlag GmbH, Kaufingerstraße 24, 80331 München, Germany